THE **ESSENTIAL** BUYER'S GUIDE

TRIUM

THUNDE

T0168170

TROPHY & TIGER

650cc & 750cc models: 1950-1983

Your marque expert:
Peter Henshaw

Essential Buyer's Guide Series
Alfa GT (Booker)
Alfa Romeo Spider Giulia (Booker & Talbott)
Audi TT (Davies)
Austin Seven (Barker)
Big Healeys (Trummel)
BMW E21 3 Series (1975-1983) (Reverente, Cook)
BMW GS (Henshaw)
BMW X5 (Saunders)
BSA 500 & 650 Twins (Henshaw)
BSA Bantam (Henshaw)
Citroën 2CV (Paxton)
Citroën ID & DS (Heilig)
Cobra Replicas (Ayre)
Corvette C2 Sting Ray 1963-1967 (Falconer)
Ducati Bevel Twins (Falloon)
Ducati Desmodue Twins (Falloon)
Ducati Desmoquattro Twins (Falloon)
Fiat 500 & 600 (Bobbitt)
Ford Capri (Paxton)
Ford Escort Mk1 & Mk2 (Williamson)
Ford Mustang (Cook)
Ford RS Cosworth Sierra & Escort (Williamson)
Harley-Davidson Big Twins (Henshaw)
Hinckley Triumph triples & fours 750, 900, 955, 1000, 1050, 1200 – 1991-2009 (Henshaw)
Honda CBR600 Hurricane (Henshaw)
Honda CBR FireBlade (Henshaw)
Honda SOHC fours 1969-1984 (Henshaw)
Jaguar E-type 3.8 & 4.2-litre (Crespin)
Jaguar E-type V12 5.3-litre (Crespin)
Jaguar XJ 1995-2003 (Crespin)
Jaguar XK8 & XKR (1996-2005) (Thorley)
Jaguar/Daimler XJ6, XJ12 & Sovereign (Crespin)
Jaguar/Daimler XJ40 (Crespin)
Jaguar Mark 1 & 2 (All models including Daimler 2.5-litre V8) 1955 to 1969 (Thorley)
Jaguar S-type – 1999 to 2007 (Thorley)
Jaguar X-type – 2001 to 2009 (Thorley)
Jaguar XJ-S (Crespin)
Jaugar XJ6, XJ8 & XJR (Thorley)
Jaguar XK 120, 140 & 150 (Thorley)
Kawasaki Z1 & Z900 (Orritt)
Land Rover Series I, II & IIA (Thurman)
Land Rover Series III (Thurman)
Lotus Seven replicas & Caterham 7: 1973-2013 (Hawkins)
Mazda MX-5 Miata (Mk1 1989-97 & Mk2 98-2001) (Crook)
Mercedes-Benz 280SL-560DSL Roadsters (Bass)
Mercedes-Benz 'Pagoda' 230SL, 250SL & 280SL
MGA 1955-1962 (Sear, Crosier)
MGF & MG TF (Hawkins)
MGB & MGB GT (Williams)
MG Midget & A-H Sprite (Horler)
MG TD, TF & TF1500 (Jones)
Mini (Paxton)
Morris Minor & 1000 (Newell)
New Mini (Collins)
Norton Commando (Henshaw)
Peugeot 205 GTI (Blackburn)
Porsche 911 (930) Turbo series (Streather)
Porsche 911 (964) (Streather)
Porsche 911 (993) (Streather)
Porsche 911 (996) (Streather)
Porsche 911 Carrera 3.2 series 1984 to 1989 (Streather)
Porsche 911SC – Coupé, Targa, Cabriolet & RS Model years 1978-1983 (Streather)
Porsche 924 – All models 1976 to 1988 (Hodgkins)
Porsche 928 (Hemmings)
Porsche 930 Turbo & 911 (930) Turbo (Streather)
Porsche 944(Higgins, Mitchell)
Porsche 986 Boxster series (Streather)
Porsche 987 Boxster and Cayman series (Streather)
Rolls-Royce Silver Shadow & Bentley T-Series (Bobbitt)
Subaru Impreza (Hobbs)
Triumph Bonneville (Henshaw)
Triumph Stag (Mort & Fox)
Triumph TR7 & TR8 (Williams)
Triumph Thunderbird, Trophy & Tiger (Henshaw)
Vespa Scooters – Classic two-stroke models 1960-2008 (Paxton)
Volvo 700/900 Series (Beavis)
VW Beetle (Cservenka & Copping)
VW Bus (Cservenka & Copping)
VW Golf GTI (Cservenka & Copping)

www.veloce.co.uk

For post publication news, updates and amendments relating to this book please visit www.veloce.co.uk/book/V4609

First published in March 2014 by Veloce Publishing Limited, Veloce House, Parkway Farm Business Park, Middle Farm Way, Poundbury, Dorchester, Dorset, DT1 3AR, England.
Fax 01305 250479/e-mail info@veloce.co.uk/web www.veloce.co.uk or www.velocebooks.com.
ISBN: 978-1-845846-09-1 UPC: 6-36847-04609-5
© Peter Henshaw and Veloce Publishing 2014. All rights reserved. With the exception of quoting brief passages for the purpose of review, no part of this publication may be recorded, reproduced or transmitted by any means, including photocopying, without the written permission of Veloce Publishing Ltd. Throughout this book logos, model names and designations, etc, have been used for the purposes of identification, illustration and decoration. Such names are the property of the trademark holder as this is not an official publication.
Readers with ideas for automotive books, or books on other transport or related hobby subjects, are invited to write to the editorial director of Veloce Publishing at the above address.
British Library Cataloguing in Publication Data – A catalogue record for this book is available from the British Library.
Typesetting, design and page make-up all by Veloce Publishing Ltd on Apple Mac. Printed in India by Imprint Digital Ltd.

Introduction
– the purpose of this book

Of all British classic bikes, perhaps none excite more interest and attention than Triumph twins. This book is a straightforward, practical guide to buying a used single-carburettor Triumph 650 or 750: Thunderbird, T110, TR6 Trophy, or Tiger. It won't list all of the correct colour combinations for each year, or analyse the bikes' design philosophy, or consider their background as part of a troubled industry – there are excellent books listed at the end of this one that do all that – but hopefully it will help you avoid buying a dud.

For years, these single-carburettor Triumph twins were the Cinderellas of Meriden – far outshone by the glamour of the twin-carb Bonneville. And yet, all that lies between these bikes are a carburettor, a name, and a little less horsepower. The riding experience, and that Triumph sense of purity and style, are almost identical. In fact, there's a lot to be said for choosing one of these twins over their more famous brother. Not only is there no need to synchronise a pair of carburettors, but the

Don't fancy a Bonneville? This Tiger 650 makes for a fine alternative.

High-pipe Trophy has desert racing heritage.

single-carb setup delivers easier starting, a more reliable tickover, more tractable low speed running, and better fuel economy. It's no accident that when the police bought Triumphs, it was the single-carburettor Saint, not the Bonneville, that was chosen.

These bikes have a long history, kicking off with the original Thunderbird of 1949: a lusty, but well-mannered, 649cc twin built in response to demands for more power from the booming export market of North America. But the Thunderbird was really a tourer, and the faster T110 soon followed. American buyers also inspired the TR6 Trophy, a dual-purpose bike that would dominate off-road racing in the States for a decade.

Through the '60s, the Trophy gradually increased in power and became a single-carburettor version of the Bonneville, but when the Tiger 750 arrived in 1973, the emphasis was on torque, lower power, and better longevity. In this guise at the Meriden workers' co-operative, the single-carb Triumph survived right until the end in 1983, though made in shrinking numbers.

Today, these single-carb Triumphs make fantastic classic bikes: the touring Thunderbird, rortier T110 or Tiger 650, the rugged high-piped Trophy, and the later Tiger 750s are all true practical classics. All look good, sound nice, and ride well.

Thanks go to H&H Auctions and Roger Fogg for their help with pictures. Also Mick and Gastair.

Contents

THE ESSENTIAL BUYER'S GUIDE™ CURRENCY

At the time of publication a BG unit of currency "●" equals approximately £1.00/US$1.62/Euro 1.20. Please adjust to suit current exchange rates using Sterling as the base currency.

1 Is it the right bike for you?
– marriage guidance

Tall and short riders
Compared to modern bikes, Triumph Thunderbird/Trophy/Tigers are relatively small and lightweight, especially by 650/750 standards. However, short riders should steer clear of the 1971 bikes with their sky-scraping 34.5in seat height.

Running costs
Surprisingly modest, as old Triumphs are not gas-guzzlers. You can expect 50mpg, and 55-60mpg when ridden gently.

Maintenance
Make no mistake, any bike from this era needs more TLC and sympathy than a modern machine. You'll need to change the oil every 1500 miles to maximise engine life, and keep an eye open for things coming loose or going out of adjustment. Not a 'ride it, forget it' sort of bike.

Kickstarting
Very few Tigers had an electric start (about 200 were built in 1981-83), but kickstarting is more about technique than strength. A well set up Triumph will not be hard to start, and the single-carb bikes are generally easier to fire up than the twin-carb Bonneville.

Usability
Need to do lots of motorway (freeway) miles or urban commuting? Not the bike for you. Triumph twins are, however, easy and very satisfying to ride on an open, twisty road.

Parts availability
Excellent, with many parts still being made. You can't build a completely new bike from all new parts, but that prospect is probably closer than with any other classic machine.

Parts costs
Very good. Because so many Triumph twins were made and are still around (some parts didn't change for years), spares aren't expensive.

Insurance group
Go for a classic bike limited mileage policy, such as that offered by Carole Nash or Footman James (in the UK) or similar insurers of classic/collectable motorcycles in other countries, and you won't pay much for insurance either.

Investment potential
The Trophy/Tiger is no longer the poor relation to the Bonneville, so prices have risen, but these bikes will hold their value now. Best buys are the 1970s Tiger 750s – the least expensive models to buy now, and likely to appreciate.

Foibles

Triumph twins vibrate and leak oil – that's part of motorcycling folklore. However, most riders aren't bothered by the vibes, which only really intrude at high revs, and a well assembled engine in good condition shouldn't leak.

Plus points

Postwar Triumph twins are one of the most cult motorcycles of all time; with good looks and torquey, punchy performance. Lightweight too, if you're used to heavier, modern bikes.

Minus points

Like any motorcycle of this era, the Trophy/Tiger needs looking after (though that can be part of the attraction), and the pre-71s are expensive especially if you just want some weekend fun.

Alternatives

The Bonneville is the closest alternative, but offers little more than the glamour of its name, twin carburettors, and slightly more performance. There are plenty of single-carb equivalents from BSA, AJS/Matchless, and Royal Enfield.

1972 Tiger 650 – easier to live with than you might think, given some TLC.

2 Cost considerations

– affordable, or a money pit?

Triumph spares, by and large, are not expensive, and Tiger 750 parts in particular are good value compared with spares for modern Japanese bikes. It's labour costs that mount up, rather than parts. If you are prepared to service the bike yourself, a Trophy/Tiger should be quite affordable to run, and at 50-60mpg, it's even quite good on fuel.

Item	Cost
Complete restoration (basket case to concours)	around x10000
Air cleaner (TR6)	x65
Alternator (Lucas RM21, stator only)	x118
Brake shoes (7in rear)	x27
Brake shoes (8in tls front)	x25
Brake pads (TR7)	x12
Brake master cylinder (TR7)	x115
Battery (12v Lucas)	x22.50
Camshafts	x85 each
Carburettor (Amal Concentric 900)	x98
Clutch chainwheel (650)	x56
Clutch centre	x104
Cylinder barrel (650, 9-stud)	x269
Downpipes (TR6, with balance pipe)	x114 pair
Electronic ignition	x85
Fork stanchions (TR6)	x76 pair
Fork stanchion shuttle valve (TR7)	x15
Gasket set	x43
Gearbox sprocket (5-speed)	x22
Headlamp shell (Lucas)	x43
Ignition switch (TR6)	x25
Mudguard (front, TR6)	x63
Mudguard (rear, Thunderbird)	x250
Oil pump (Morgo)	x88
Rear chain (Renolds)	x50
Pistons (TR7)	x78 pair
Primary chain (TR6)	x42
Rear shocks	x101 pair
Seat (6T, TR6, complete)	x145
Silencers (6T)	x215 pair
Speedometer (reconditioned)	x263
Tank badge (Thunderbird)	x49 each
Valves	x18 each
Wiring loom (TR6)	x66

Trophy/Tigers share many parts with other Triumphs ...

... most parts are available new.

3 Living with a Triumph twin

– will you get along together?

The single-carburettor Triumph 650s and 750s have a reputation for being easier to live with than the twin-carburettor Bonneville. True, they don't have two carburettors to balance, and enjoy better manners at low speeds, but they are still bikes from a very different era. Back in the 1960s, plenty of riders used these Triumph twins as everyday transport, but they tended to be Belstaff-clad young bloods who were keen enough to take on the intensive maintenance that went with it (or happy to live with the oil leaks and unreliability that resulted from neglect). Today, consumer products keep working without much attention – it's an age where bikes need only an oil check and chain tweak between major services, but old bikes aren't like that. Triumph twins demand a lot more looking after.

Tiger 750 is a less demanding bike to own. (Courtesy Mick – Creative Commons)

Having said all that, generally speaking, the later the model the easier it is to live with, and some folk do use later machines as everyday transport, though for most, a Triumph of this era is a second bike: kept in the garage for sunny days. Even then, it demands a different mindset to riding a modern bike. The relationship is based on constant awareness of how the bike is running ... has that nut vibrated loose? Is that the beginnings of a leak from the rocker box? If an indicator ceases to function, is it the bulb or just a loose connector?

All these little things are part of classic bike ownership, and many owners would say they are part of what makes owning an older Triumph twin (or indeed most old bikes) more satisfying than a new machine. You develop a relationship with it that is quite different to that with a bike that always starts on the button and never goes wrong.

The single-carburettor Triumph 650s and 750s include a wide range of machines from the first Thunderbird in 1949 to the final Tiger 750 in 1983. There were lots

Late 1960s bikes enjoyed several improvements – this is a '68.

of changes during that time, usually improvements that make a bike easier to live with. The pre-unit construction bikes (made up to 1962) do have poorer brakes than the later machines – not to mention six-volt dynamo or magneto electrics – but the Thunderbird and early Trophy are in a mild state of tune – torquey and flexible. The higher compression Tiger 110 was faster, with a better front brake.

The unit construction 650s (1963-70) saw the Trophy and Tiger change character, as Triumph continually increased power in an effort to keep up with horsepower demand from the USA and the encroaching Japanese competition. Some say Triumphs (the Bonneville in particular) were over-tuned in the process, but this is really outweighed by the practical advances: 12-volt electrics, better brakes and lubrication, a stiffer, better handling frame, and more thorough breathing to combat oil leaks. All of these things make the later Trophys and Tigers less demanding to own than the earlier ones.

Of course, there's nothing to stop an owner fitting lower compression pistons and milder cams, and it all really depends on how serious you are about originality. Alternatively, you could search for one of the 1963-66 Thunderbirds, which kept their lower state of tune, though these are rare.

When the Tiger 650 became a 750 in 1973, its character changed again, and these final-era Tigers are arguably the easiest to live with of all. Don't be put off by the larger capacity; the first Tiger 750 wasn't much heavier than the 650, physically no bigger, and had a lower seat than the '71 650s. Just as important, Triumph had finally accepted that its venerable twin couldn't keep up with the Japanese fours, and de-tuned it with milder cams and lower compression. The result was more low and mid-range torque than the highly-strung 650, and better flexibility at low speed. One of these will happily cruise at 65-70mph, two-up with luggage.

As with the earlier bikes, steady improvements were made over the years, such as electronic ignition, timing-side roller bearing and high-output alternator in 1979, and a four-valve oil pump the following year. These are all good, pragmatic changes that make the Triumphs easier to run day-to-day, and, because the bikes didn't change fundamentally, it's possible to apply them retrospectively to older machines. Purists might protest about originality, but many of these improvements don't affect the bike's appearance at all. Once again, it's all down to what sort of riding you intend to do, how happy you are with fettling, and whether you're a stickler for complete originality.

Otherwise, a Trophy/Tiger can be made very easy to live with, especially if you're prepared to sacrifice a little unseen originality. But whatever you do, it will never be a 'push button and ride' sort of bike.

Triumphs are easy on the eye.

4 Relative values
– which model for you?

See Chapter 12 for value assessment. This chapter shows, in relative percentage terms, the value of individual models in good condition. There were many variations on the Trophy/Tiger theme over its long production life, and this chapter also looks at the strengths and weaknesses of each model, so that you can decide which is best for you. Basically, the bikes' evolution can be divided into five stages.

Range

1959-62 Pre-unit 650s – Thunderbird, TR6, T110
1963-70 Unit 650s – Thunderbird, Trophy, Tiger 650
1971-74 Oil-in-frame 650s – Trophy, Tiger 650
1973-77 Early Meriden 750s – Tiger 750
1978-83 Late Meriden 750s – Tiger 750

1959-62 Pre-unit 650s

The original Thunderbird of 1949 was Triumph's first postwar 650, and came with a mild 7:1 compression ratio and cast iron cylinder head and barrel, but the extra capacity (649cc) boosted power to 34bhp at 6300rpm. Otherwise, it was a continuation of the 500cc Speed Twin, with the same cycle parts and four-speed gearbox.

That meant rudimentary rear suspension from Triumph's sprung hub, which gave limited travel to an otherwise rigid rear end. A very economical SU carburettor was fitted from 1951, and swinging arm frame from 1957.

Later Thunderbirds (this is a '61) acquired extra bodywork.

Like all Triumphs of that period, the Thunderbird had a real sense of style – the almost symmetrical lines topped by the elegant headlamp nacelle. Later T'birds (along with other Triumphs) acquired the 'bathtub' bodywork, which partially enclosed the rear wheel, making it a real period piece.

In 1953, the Thunderbird was joined by the more sporting T110, with swinging arm frame, high-compression pistons, different camshafts and larger carburettor – the engine changes boosted power to 42bhp. Road tests reported a top speed of over 110mph, and in 1956 an alloy cylinder head, higher compression and eight-inch ventilated front brake were added.

Period shot of an early Thunderbird in Cornwall, UK. Add some luggage and they're ready to tour!

The same year, the TR6 Trophy was launched. This was based on the T110, but with high-level exhaust, smaller fuel tank, detachable headlight and larger rear tyre, was aimed at the off-road market in the US. A great success in the States, it helped assure Triumph's dominance of US off-road competition (especially desert racing) for a decade. From 1960 it was offered in low-pipe road form as well, effectively taking over from the T110 as a sort-of single-carburettor version of the Bonneville. Most collectable of these early Trophies though, are the high-piped bikes, with their rugged off-road looks. These are rare in the UK, as most were exported to the US.

The faster, high-compression T110 was a sportier take on the T'bird.

Strengths/weaknesses: Soft, touring power delivery on the Thunderbird, and pre-Bonneville performance from T110. 1950s Triumph style. Weak brakes, electrics not as reliable as later 12-volt alternator system, and maintenance is more demanding (eg adjusting the primary drive involves moving the gearbox within the frame).
104%

1963-70 unit 650s

The 1960s was Triumph's boom time, with thousands of bikes rolling off the Meriden production lines, many of them exported to the US. Although the Bonneville was the flagship bike, the Trophy was part of this success, and, on the West Coast, the off-road version was actually equal best-seller with the Bonneville, reflecting the greater popularity of off-road competition on that side of the States.

Throughout the '60s, there were two basic versions of the Trophy: road going TR6R or TR6SS (road tyres and low-level exhaust), and the off-road TR6C or SC (Dunlop Trials Universal tyres and high pipes). Of course, for all their off-road style, these Trophys were road-legal, and many were used as pure road bikes. The Thunderbird line continued, though, with the market's increased emphasis on sports rather than touring, sold in smaller numbers. The road Trophy was renamed Tiger 650 from 1969.

For some, a 1960s unit construction Triumph is the pick of the bunch.

Trophy engines gained a higher state of tune in the '60s.

This 1968 Trophy includes many useful upgrades.

All of these bikes came in unit construction form – that is, with the engine and gearbox built in one piece. They were cheaper to make, could use an alternator, and had a cleaner appearance than the pre-unit. A new nine-stud head sought to prevent cracking, and a new single downtube frame was stiffer and handled better than the last of the pre-units. More chassis changes (a different steering head angle, and better swing arm support from 1966) turned the unit 650 Triumphs into some of the best handling bikes of the time.

In fact, 1966 was a key year for change for all Triumph 650/750s, with 12-volt electrics, better lubrication, a bigger oil tank, and a new front brake with 44 per cent more shoe area, as well as frame improvements. An eight-inch twin leading shoe front brake and two-way damped forks followed in '68. Some think that the 1969-70 Triumphs are the peak of the breed, incorporating all of these changes, but without the troubles affecting early oil-in-frame bikes.

For the Trophy in particular (the Thunderbird was dropped in 1966), this period saw an increasing state of tune, as the bike effectively became a single-carburettor Bonneville. It had already acquired the Bonnie's sporting E3134 inlet cam in 1959 and increased 8.5:1 compression in 1961. A bigger Amal carburettor followed in '64, with bigger valves, stronger springs, and R-type cam followers in '66. In 1968, now with a 9.0:1 compression ratio, it got the Bonneville E3134 exhaust cam as well.

Strengths/weaknesses: Better frame, electrics, and brakes, especially from 1966, make the unit 650 Trophys particularly attractive. Still fast, but with more refinement than the pre-unit machines. However, ever increasing demands for power also brought more vibration.

100%

1971-74 oil-in-frame 650s

Less revered (at least in the UK) than the earlier bikes (though the early 1970s Tiger and Trophy 650 are also rare in the UK, as many were exported). Unveiled for 1971 and launched as part of a major update to the entire range, they had an all-new frame, forks, and (big step, this) flashing indicators. But it proved to be a disaster – the new frame, using its large top tube as an oil tank, was prone to fractures, allowed the engine to run hot, and forced a massive seat height of 34.5in. The new conical hub drum brakes were poor, and the bikes' skimpy mudguards and

Disliked by some, but the early oil-in-frame 650s have their own style.

exposed fork stanchions were clearly aimed at West Coast USA rather than damp UK.

However, the oil-in-frame 650s did settle down after a while. The frame, for all its faults, handled well, and from mid-1972 the seat was lowered to a more practical 31.5in. That year also brought an optional five-speed gearbox (making the bike a TR6RV) which was interchangeable with the old cluster. As before, there were two basic versions: the TR6C Trophy 650, and TR6R Tiger 650. The main difference between them was low- or high-level exhaust. The Trophy had become a street scrambler rather than a genuine dual-purpose bike, and was dropped in early 1972. This left the Tiger 650 on its own, gaining a front disc brake for 1973, though production ceased with the blockade of the Meriden factory in June of that year.

Strengths/weaknesses: The early oil-in-frame Trophy/Tigers certainly had their weaknesses, and some still consider them to be an inferior bike. However, they do have a certain style, and most of the frame's teething troubles were ironed out by 1973, when the disc brake was a worthwhile addition.

71%

1972 Tiger 650, with US styling.

1973-78 early Tiger 750s

Launched in 1973 alongside the Bonneville 750, the biggest Tiger reflected the increasing popularity of the 750cc sector. It was no faster than the 650, and, in fact, top end power was slightly down. To allow the venerable twin to cope with its bigger capacity, Triumph de-tuned it, with lower compression and milder cams. The result was a flexible, torquey machine, though vibration was worse. It also had a ten-stud cylinder-head.

1972 Tiger 650 in UK form – lower bars and bigger fuel tank.

The 750 is less stressed and more torquey than the 650.

Like the 650, it came in US and UK forms, and from mid-1975 changed to a left-foot gear change (dictated by US regulations). Other key changes were a rear disc brake and improved Lucas switchgear from 1976, and better sealing for the forks and front wheel bearings from '78.

Strengths/weaknesses: More robust than the 650, a torquey and pleasant machine to ride, though vibration is more noticeable. Lacks style of earlier bikes, and rarely comes up for sale. The cheapest route to Tiger ownership.
69%

1979-83 later Tiger 750s

The final Meriden-built Triumphs are often referred to as practical classics, and with good reason – they developed over the years into well-sorted bikes that give enjoyable, trouble-free riding. No one pretended that these were performance bikes anymore: now they were more about the riding experience than sheer performance.

However, stricter emissions laws outlawed the Tiger from being exported to the US. While the Bonneville was modified to cope, the Tiger's smaller sales meant it wasn't worthwhile. Regardless, the Tiger did share in the Bonnie's many improvements for 1979.

Early 750s are the cheapest of all Trophy/Tigers.

That year, the crank was more thoroughly machined to reduce vibration, and gained an SKF roller bearing on the timing side. Lucas Rita electronic ignition was another big step forward, giving a more accurate spark that didn't slip out of time, as was a high-output three-phase alternator and clearer switchgear.

Although the Meriden co-operative was desperately short of money, it still made strenuous efforts to keep improving the bikes. 1980 saw a new four-valve oil pump (which greatly improved both pumping and scavenging capacity), easier primary chain adjustment, and repositioned rear brake caliper (the previous underslung caliper was vulnerable to road grit and corrosion). The big change for 1981 was an electric start option; fitted to around half the Triumphs.

Variations on the single-carb Tiger theme arrived in 1982. The Tiger Trail was a dual-purpose bike, with 21-inch front wheel, Avon Mudplugger tyres and high-level exhaust. It created quite an impact (especially in the bright yellow colour scheme), but few were made

A nice, clean (later) 750. Ribbed 'points' cover denotes electronic ignition.

Sharing improvements with the Bonneville, the Tiger 750 can make for a practical day-to-day bike.

so it's a real collector's item now. Another new variant was the TR65 Thunderbird, Triumph's first 650 since 1973, and an attempt to produce a cheaper bike, using a short-stroke 649cc version of the 750. As with the Tiger Trail it's a rare beast, as less than 500 were made. For 1983, it was listed in Tiger Trail form as well. German buyers can keep an eye open for the very rare TR27, of which just 26 were made in 1979-80. These were restricted 27bhp versions of the Tiger 750, built to take advantage of lower insurance rates in Germany for bikes of that power.

Strengths/weaknesses: The later Tiger 750 is a good choice for regular use. It's a little down on power compared with earlier 750s, but is smoother and more refined, plus better on fuel. Meriden's quality control improved at this time, though like any Triumph twin, the Tiger does need a sympathetic owner. About half the final Triumphs were fitted with electric start, and 25 years on, any teething troubles should have been sorted. Tiger Trail doesn't have the style of earlier TR6C Trophys, but does have rarity value, as does the TR65 Thunderbird. Even standard Tiger 750s are hard to find compared to the much more common Bonneville T140.
73%

US- or UK-spec?

Later Tigers are usually referred to as being in US- or UK-spec – a reflection of the vital importance of the North American market to Triumph. There are few differences, the main ones being the style of fuel tank and handlebars – US-spec bikes came with high bars and a pretty, slimline 2.5- or 3-gallon fuel tank; UK bikes had a slab-sided 4-gallon tank and lower bars. Both styles were offered in Britain from 1973, though, of course, many US-spec bikes have since been imported. Which is best is in the eye of the beholder, and whether you prefer a laid back or slightly lean forward riding position. The US bikes are arguably prettier, the UK ones have a longer tank range. In terms of price, there's no real difference.

The Tiger Trail was an attempt to rival BMW's R80 G/S. (Courtesy Gastair)

5 Before you view
– be well informed

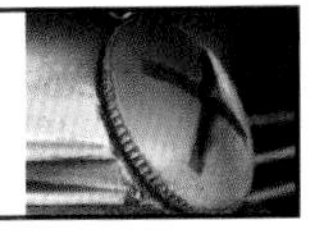

To avoid a wasted journey, and the disappointment of finding that the bike does not match your expectations, it will help if you're very clear about what questions you want to ask before you pick up the phone. Some of these points might appear basic, but when you're excited about the prospect of buying your dream classic, it's amazing how some of the most obvious things slip the mind ... Also check the current values of the model you are interested in the classic bike magazine classified ads.

Where is the bike?
Is it going to be worth travelling to the next county/state, or even across a border? A locally-advertised machine, although it may not sound very interesting, can add to your knowledge for very little effort, so make a visit – it might even be in better condition than you expect.

Dealer or private sale?
Establish early on if the bike is being sold by its owner or by a trader. A private owner should have all the history, so don't be afraid to ask detailed questions. A dealer may have more limited knowledge of the bike's history, but should have some documentation. A dealer may offer a warranty/guarantee (ask for a printed copy).

Cost of collection and delivery?
A dealer may well be used to quoting for delivery. A private owner may agree to meet you halfway, but only agree to this after you have seen the bike at the vendor's address to validate the documents. Conversely, you could meet halfway and agree the sale, but insist on meeting at the vendor's address for the handover.

View – when and where?
It is always preferable to view at the vendor's home or business premises. In the case of a private sale, the bike's documentation should tally with the vendor's name and address. Arrange to view only in daylight, and avoid a wet day – the vendor may be reluctant to let you take a test ride if it's wet.

Reason for sale?
Do make it one of the first questions. Why is the bike being sold and how long has it been with the current owner? How many previous owners?

Condition?
Ask for an honest appraisal of the bike's condition. Ask specifically about some of the check items described in Chapter 9.

All original specification?
A completely original Trophy/Tiger will be worth more than a modified one, but certain mods (later oil pump, electronic ignition) can also indicate a conscientious owner who has been actively riding/caring for the machine.

Matching data/legal ownership?

Do frame, engine numbers and licence plate match the official registration document? Is the owner's name and address recorded in the official registration documents?

For those countries that require an annual test of roadworthiness, does the bike have a document showing it complies (an MOT certificate in the UK, which can be verified on 0845 600 5977)?

If it's a 1973 or later bike, does it carry a current road fund license/licence plate tag? Earlier bikes are road tax exempt in the UK.

Does the vendor own the bike outright? Money might be owed to a finance company or bank: the bike could even be stolen. Several organisations will supply the data on ownership, based on the bike's licence plate number, for a fee. Such companies can often also tell you whether the bike has been 'written off' by an insurance company. In the UK these organisations can supply vehicle data:

HPI - 01722 422 422 – www.hpicheck.com
AA - 0870 600 0836 – www.theaa.com
RAC - 0870 533 3660 – www.rac.co.uk
Other countries will have similar organisations.

Unleaded fuel?

Has the bike been modified to run on unleaded fuel?

Insurance?

Check with your existing insurer before setting out – your current policy might not cover you if you do buy the bike and decide to ride it home.

How you can pay?

A cheque/check will take several days to clear and the seller may prefer to sell to a cash buyer. However, a banker's draft (a cheque issued by a bank) is as good as cash, but safer, so contact your own bank and become familiar with the formalities that are necessary to obtain one.

Buying at auction?

If the intention is to buy at auction see Chapter 10 for further advice.

Professional vehicle check (mechanical examination)

There are often marque/model specialists who will undertake professional examination of a vehicle on your behalf. Owners clubs may be able to put you in touch with such specialists.

VISIT VELOCE ON THE WEB – WWW.VELOCE.CO.UK
All current books • New book news • Special offers • Gift vouchers • Forum

6 Inspection equipment
– these items will really help

Inspection equipment
This book
Reading glasses (if you need them for close work)
Overalls
Camera
Compression tester
A friend, preferably a knowledgeable enthusiast

Before you rush out of the door, gather together a few items that will help as you work your way around the bike. This book is designed to be your guide at every step, so take it along and use the check boxes in Chapter 9 to help you assess each area of the bike you're interested in. Don't be afraid to let the seller see you using it.

Take your reading glasses if you need them to read documents and make close up inspections.

Be prepared to get dirty. Take along a pair of overalls, if you have them.

If you have use of a camera, take it along so that later you can study some areas of the bike more closely. Take a picture of any part of the bike that causes you concern, and seek a friend's opinion.

A compression tester is easy to use. It screws into the sparkplug holes, and on a Trophy/Tiger these couldn't be easier to get to. With the ignition off, turn the engine over on full throttle (sparkplugs removed) to get the compression reading.

Ideally, have a friend or knowledgeable enthusiast accompany you: a second opinion is always valuable.

7 Fifteen minute evaluation
– walk away or stay?

Spotting a hybrid

However good the condition of the bike, however well it's been restored, there's not much point in going any further if it's pretending to be something it isn't. For example, it's easy to dress up a road-going TR6R as the rarer TR6C, simply by adding high-level pipes.

The truth should be revealed by the engine number, stamped on the left-hand side just below the cylinder barrel. Numbers should be clear: any 'fuzzy' numbers could be a sign of tampering. Later machines had this area stamped with the Triumph logo to make tampering more difficult. The model code ('TR6C,' TR6SS' etc) will be stamped on the left of the engine/frame number.

First, check the engine numbers – this is a genuine TR6SS.

Now look for the frame number, on the left-hand side of the headstock. This should carry the same number as the engine. If not, the bike has had a different engine fitted at some point. There may have been a good reason for this, so finding non-matching numbers doesn't necessarily mean it's time to walk away. The bike itself may still be an honest machine with plenty to offer – you just need to make it clear to the seller that you know it isn't 100 per cent original and start negotiating on price.

Documentation

If the seller claims to be the bike's owner, make sure he/she really is by checking the registration document, which, in the UK, is the V5C. The person listed on the V5C isn't necessarily the legal owner, but the details should match those of whomever is selling the bike. Also use the V5C to check the engine/frame numbers.

An annual roadworthiness certificate – the 'MOT' in the UK – is handy proof that the bike was roadworthy when tested. A whole sheaf of them gives evidence of the bike's history – when it was

General impressions are important, but look behind the gloss.

actively being used, and what the mileage was. The more of these that come with the bike, the better. Bikes built before 1960 no longer require an MOT in the UK.

General condition

Put the bike on its centre stand, to shed equal light on both sides, and take a good, slow walk around it. If it's claimed to be restored, and has a nice shiny tank and engine cases, look more closely – how far does the 'restored' finish go? Are the nooks and crannies behind the gearbox as spotless as the fuel tank? If not, the bike may have been given a quick smarten up to sell. A generally faded look all over isn't necessarily a bad thing – it suggests a machine that hasn't been restored, and isn't trying to pretend that it has.

Now look at the engine – by far the most expensive and time-consuming thing to put right if anything's wrong. A lot of people will have told you that all old Triumphs leak oil, but there shouldn't be any serious leaks if the engine is in good condition and has been put together well. It shouldn't be spattered with lube, or have oily drips underneath. Even if it's dry on top, get down on your knees and have a peek at the underside of the crankcase – nice and dry, or covered in oil? A light misting here and there is nothing to worry about.

Take the bike off the centre stand and start the engine – it should fire up within two or three kicks, and rev up crisply and cleanly without showing blue or black smoke. Some top end clatter is normal, but listen for rumbles and knocks from the bottom end, and clonks from the primary drive – any of these are indicators of serious work being required. While the engine's running, check that the ignition light or ammeter show the electrics are charging, and that the oil light (on Tiger 750s) goes out.

Switch off the engine and put the bike back on its centre stand. Check for play in the forks, headstock and swingarm. Are there oil leaks from the front forks or rear shocks? Are details like the seat, badges and tank colour right for the year of the bike? (A little research helps here, and the reference books listed at the end of this volume have this information).

This 1962 TR6 looks good – no leaks, and not pretending to be concours.

8 Key points

– where to look for problems

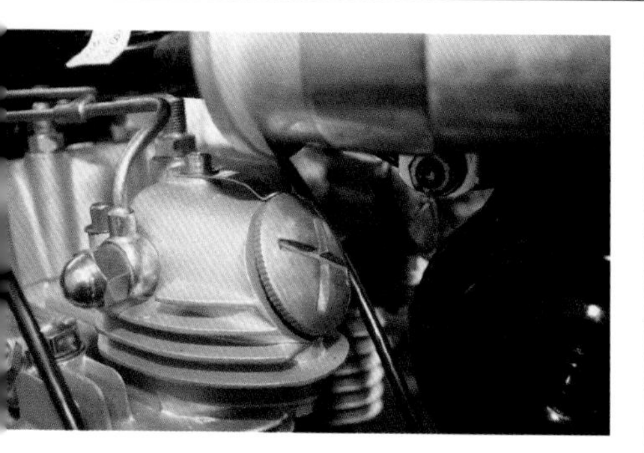

Are the bolt heads chewed or rounded-off? Is there damage to casings around bolt heads? Has someone attacked fixings with a hammer and chisel? All are sure signs of a careless previous owner with more enthusiasm than skill, coupled with a dash of impatience. Not a good sign.

Listen to the engine running. Clonks or rumbles from the bottom end indicate the main or big-end bearings are worn.

Are the engine and frame numbers correct for the year of the bike? Do they confirm that it's a genuine TR6SS or TR7RV? If not, you may still be looking at a complete, usable bike, but it won't be worth as much as a genuine machine. Note the T120 code denotes a Bonneville, not a Trophy.

Minor oil leaks aren't a major problem (though they are a bargaining point), but serious ones suggest mechanical problems or neglect.

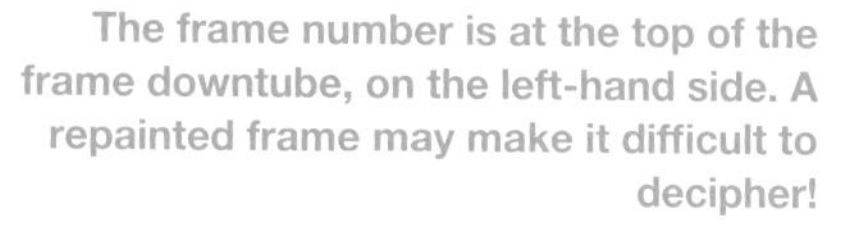

The frame number is at the top of the frame downtube, on the left-hand side. A repainted frame may make it difficult to decipher!

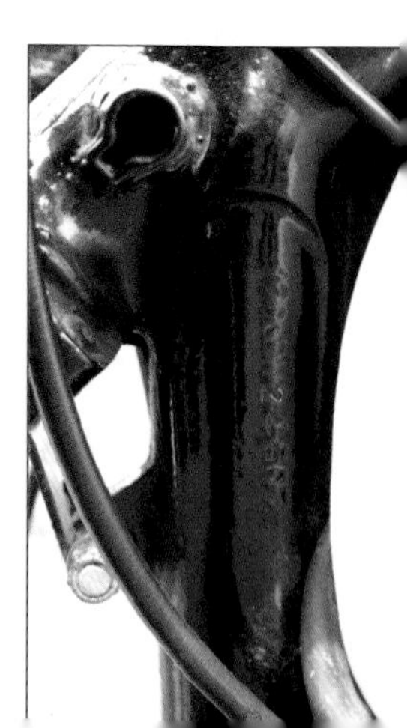

9 Serious evaluation

– 30 minutes for years of enjoyment

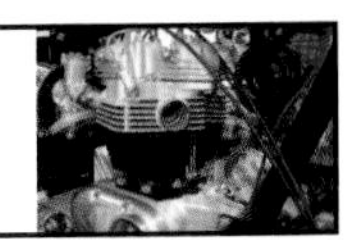

Circle the Excellent (4), Good (3), Average (2) or Poor (1) box of each section as you go along. The totting up procedure is detailed at the end of the chapter. Be realistic in your marking!

Engine/frame numbers

4 3 2 1

Engine and frame numbers should be the first thing you look at – they'll tell you whether the bike really is the model it's advertised to be, and whether the engine (or frame) is the original. Many Triumphs are advertised with 'matching numbers,' because the engine and frame numbers are the same and therefore left the factory together.

The engine number is stamped on the left-hand side, just below the cylinder barrel: easy to find and to read. The figures should be clear and not 'fuzzy' – if they aren't the number could have been tampered with, in which case walk away. The model code ('TR6R,' 'T110,' etc) will be stamped to the left of the number, so check that this agrees with the seller's description – model codes, with their production years, are listed in Chapter 17.

Now look for the frame number, stamped on the left-hand side of the headstock. This may be more difficult to read, especially if the frame has been repainted or powder coated, but it should still be visible. All the same comments apply. Most of this information is stated in the 15 min check. It's worth noting that if the frame and engine numbers don't match, the bike may still be honest and usable, but being non-original should be reflected in the price.

Check engine number and model code first.

Do the crankcase numbers match?

Model code 'TR6RV' denotes 1972/3 Tiger 650, five-speed gearbox.

Finally, check that these numbers match those on the registration document. If they don't, then it really is time to walk away.

Paint

4 3 2 1

Triumphs have always been good-looking bikes, and the paintwork makes a big contribution. The good news is that there's not that much of it, just tank, side panels and mudguards – many later 750s had chromed rather than painted mudguards, with plain black side panels, making a repaint easier still. Having said that, don't underestimate the cost of a professional job, which is well worth having done, as the fuel tank in particular is such a focal point of the whole bike. Look for evidence of quick and cheap resprays, with pinstriping, for example, that doesn't line up with the tank badges. Light staining around the filler cap, from spilt fuel, might polish out, but could also require a respray. Generally, faded original paintwork isn't necessarily a bad thing. In fact, some riders prefer this unrestored look – there are so many restored Triumphs around that an honest-looking original, even if a little faded around the edges, has its own appeal.

Tank paint finish makes a big difference.

Most Trophy/Tigers of the 1960s and early '70s had some sort of two-tone colour scheme, and for originality it's important to get the right one for the year of the bike, along with its correct pinstriping. The reference books listed at the end of this one will give you a complete listing. Paint availability shouldn't be a problem, as there are often modern equivalents – Triumph Pacific Blue from the '60s, for example (used on the TR6 for 1966), is the same as a Ford metallic blue.

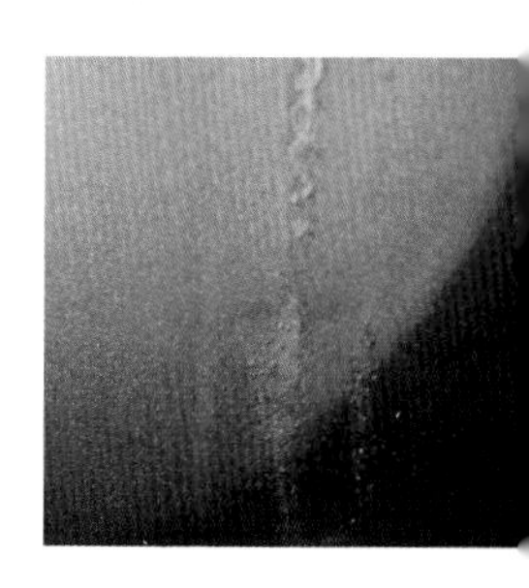

Faults like this will require a respray.

Chrome

Chrome plating is another big visual plus on these Triumphs, used on the silencers, headlamp shell, handlebars, parcel grid, mirrors, some mudguards, tank badges, and other parts. The quality of Meriden's original plating is generally pretty good, though we are talking 30 or 40 years on now, so don't expect it to be pristine.

Whichever bike you're looking at, check the chrome for rust, pitting and general dullness. Minor blemishes can be polished away, otherwise you're looking at a replating bill. If the silencers are seriously rotted, it's a better idea to budget for a new pair – less hassle than getting the old ones replated, in any case.

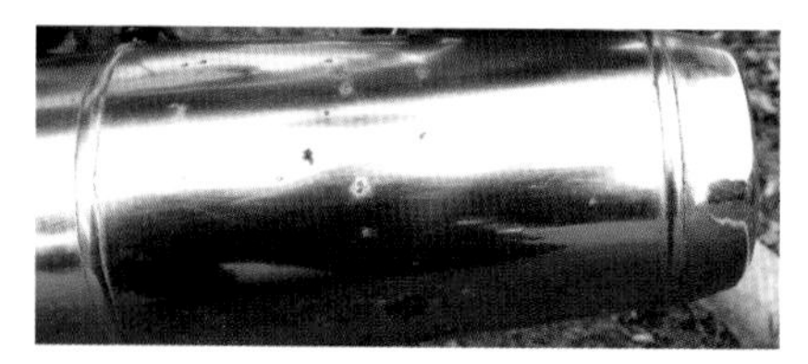

Minor rust pitting isn't immediately obvious.

Bluing of exhaust downpipes is nothing to worry about.

Tinwork

In one respect, buying a secondhand bike is usually far easier than purchasing a used car – there's far less bodywork to worry about. In the case of some Triumph twins, that's not quite so true. The Thunderbird and T110 were fitted with Triumph's elegant headlight nacelle, which should be free of dents and rust. More radical bodywork was fitted to the same bikes from 1960, such as the 'bathtub' rear end. Many of these were thrown away by 1960s riders who really wanted a café racer, but some survived. Again, check for rust. None of the TR6 Trophys were fitted with this extra bodywork.

Mudguards too, should be straight, free of rust around the rims, and securely bolted to the bike. The front mudguard stays varied in detail over the years: substantial twin stays through the 1960s; spindly rubber-mounted stays for 1971-72; and a return to a stronger type from '73.

Don't forget to check the condition of mudguards.

Up to 1970, the side panels were rounded black items, the right-hand one acting as an oil tank, and the matching left-hand one housing the toolkit. The oil tank should be checked for leaks through the seams, as repair entails removal and flushing out before it can be put right. From 1971 on, the side panels were flat (still in plain black), and covers only, as the oil tank was now part of the frame. Until 1978, these panels came in two pieces – don't expect them to line up precisely!

Headlamp nacelle on Thunderbird and T110.

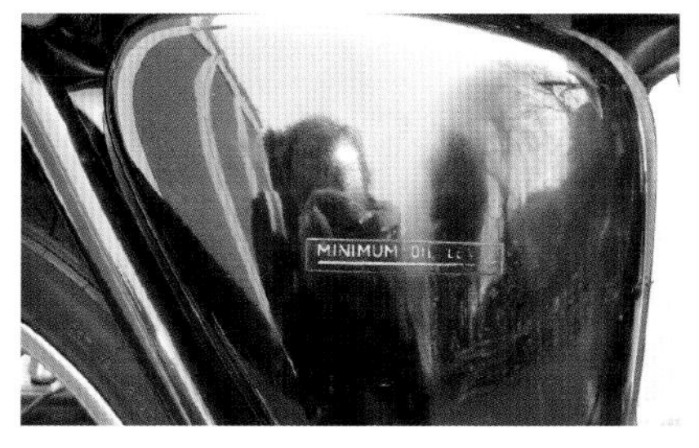

The oil tank may be dented, or leaky, or both!

The fuel tank needs to be checked for leaks around the tap and along the seams, as well as dents and rust. Watch out for patches of filler. As with the early oil tank, repairing leaks means flushing out the tank (which has to be

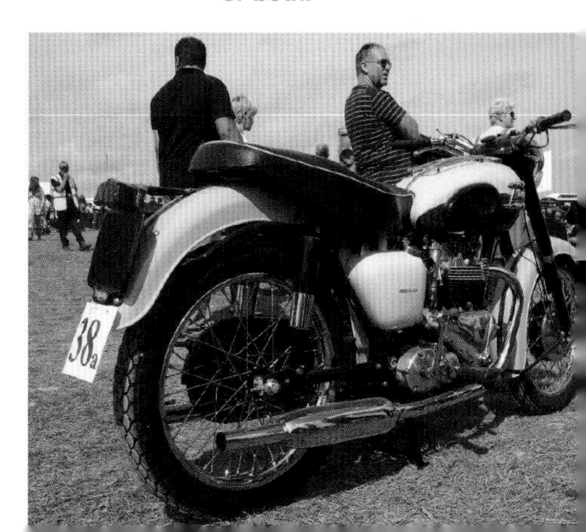

This is a '59 Bonneville, but the fuel tank and valanced mudguards were shared with the Thunderbird and T110.

thorough – you don't want any petrol vapour hanging about when the welding torch is fired up), but the fuel tank is at least easier to remove. Pinhole leaks can often be cured by Petseal, but anything more serious needs a proper repair. If the tank is beyond saving, new ones in both US and UK style are available, though once it's been painted, that's not a cheap option. So a very poor condition tank is a good bargaining lever.

Triumph's million-dollar grin – tank badges are a focal point.

Trim

These Triumphs were not fitted with over-elaborate trim, usually consisting of just the tank badges and side panel badges. Tank badges come in various styles, according to year: backed by three horizontal bars on the early Thunderbird, the grille-style badge up to 1965; the 'eyebrow' in '66-68; and the less elaborate 'picture frame' badge from '69. UK-spec 750s always had a simple 'Triumph' script, while the US-spec bikes retained the '69-on one, until 1979, when they too adopted the simple script. Whatever the badge, it should be firmly in place, with unpitted chrome and flake-free paint. All these tank badges are available new.

Pre-1971 bikes had more trim on the fuel tank, notably a chrome strip down the centre to hide the upper seam. They also had the infamous

The tank-top parcel grid was a period 1960s fitting.

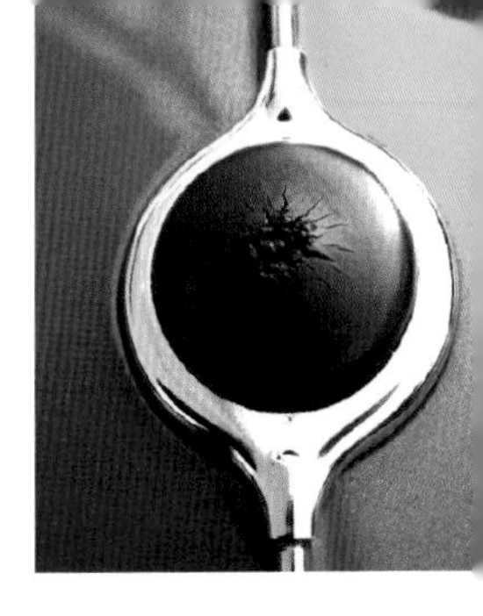

Some minor trim parts may be tricky to replace.

parcel grid, designed to allow the rider to carry small items on top of the tank. Triumph stopped fitting this traditional item in 1969, after a celebrated (if that's the right word) case in which an American rider sued the company after being emasculated by his Triumph's parcel grid during a collision. So, originality or (for male riders) personal safety – the choice is yours. If it's there, the grid should be securely mounted, with chrome in good condition.

Seat

4 3 2 1

All Trophys/Tigers had a dual seat, even those ostensibly destined for American desert racing. The exception was the police-spec TR6P, which came with a solo seat. From 1962 the dual seat neatly hinged up to reveal (depending on year) the battery, toolkit and oil filler.

There was a wide variation of styles, and once again, if originality is important, you'll need to have the right one. Pre-unit bikes had a plain black seat with white piping, though in their last year (1962), this changed to a two-tone finish of grey top and black sides. The smooth grey plastic was quilted for 1967, ribbed from 1968, and in 1971 replaced with a plain black ribbed seat, which was thinner for 1972 in an attempt to reduce seat height. A grabstrap was optional on some TR6s, with a proper grabrail fitted from 1969.

Whichever seat the bike has, the points to look for are the same. The metal pan can rust, which will eventually give way, though this is easy to check. Covers can split, which of course allows in rain, which the foam padding soaks up…and never dries out. That's a recipe for a permanently wet backside, or a rock hard seat on frosty mornings (the author speaks from experience). New covers and complete seats in various styles are available, though recovering an old seat is a specialist job.

1968 seat with grey ribbed top and grey piping.

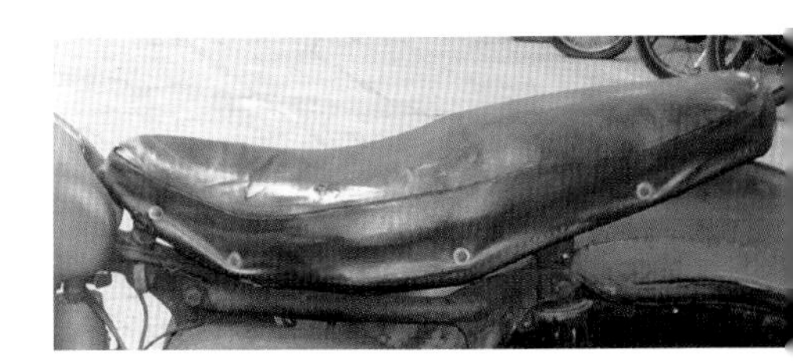

This seat may need some work …

This late model seat will need recovering.

Rubbers

Worn footrest rubbers are a good sign of high mileage, though as they're so cheap and easy to replace, not an infallible one. They should be secure on the footrest and free of splits or tears. If the footrest itself is bent upwards, that's a sure sign the bike

Check that footrest and gearlever rubbers are secure.

Worn footrest rubbers can be a sign of high mileage.

has been down the road at some point, so look for other telltale signs on that side. The kickstart and gear change rubbers are also easy to replace, so well worn ones could indicate neglect. On kickstart bikes, beware the worn smooth rubber – your foot's liable to slip off while kicking the bike over, with painful results as the kickstart lever slams back into your leg. The rubber should also be firm on the lever and not drop off after half a dozen kicks. Of course, if the engine needs that many kicks to fire it up, then something's wrong there anyway.

Frame

There were five basic types of frame, all conventional tubular steel. The Thunderbird used a single downtube type with a rigid rear end until 1955, and swingarm frame from '56. The T110 and TR6 used that frame from the start of production, and in 1960 all bikes changed to a duplex frame (twin downtubes) which delivered better handling and was stiffened further for '61 by an extra tube, though this had the side effect of increasing vibration.

Unit construction in 1963 saw a return to a single downtube frame with a well-braced swingarm support. Changes to this frame for 1966 turned all Triumph 650s into some of the best handling bikes of their time. Finally, all-new for 1971 was the oil-in-frame design, carrying engine oil in the large top tube. Early examples had trouble with fractures and oil leaks, but soon settled down – all '71-on bikes used this frame.

The only cure for paint in this condition, if you can't live with it, is a strip down and repaint.

A restored frame makes for a subtle improvement.

Check exhaust brackets aren't cracked.

A really shabby frame necessitates a strip down and repaint, though, as with the other paintwork, if it's original and fits in with the patina of the bike, then there's a good case for leaving it as it is.

Look for bent brackets, which can be heated and bent back into shape, and cracks around them, which can be welded. Those for horn and exhaust pipes are usually the first to succumb to vibration.

The most important job is to check whether the main frame is straight and true. Crash damage may have bent it, putting the wheels out of line. One way of checking is with an experienced eye, string, and a straight edge, but the surest way to ascertain a frame's straightness is on the test ride – any serious misalignment should be obvious in the way the bike handles.

Stands

4 3  2  1

All bikes were fitted with both centre and side stands, though some owners removed the centre stand to improve cornering clearance – an issue that especially affected the Tiger 750 on the left-hand side. If the stand's still there, scrape marks indicate a history of hard riding. Not that this is a problem – the Tiger is an agile bike that encourages spirited riding, and scraped stands do not necessarily equal lunatic owners.

Both stands should be secure, but especially watch 1963-67 side stands – the mounting clamp doesn't reach right around the frame tube, and this is a weak point. When on the centre stand, the bike shouldn't wobble or lean – a sign of serious stand wear and/or imminent collapse. This affects bikes which have been started and left

1963-67 side stands had weak frame clamps, but otherwise, all stands are strong and secure.

idling on the centre stand – all the vibration is transmitted to ground via the stand, which doesn't do it much good.

Lights

Triumph electrics improved dramatically with a 12-volt system in 1966, and a high-output alternator in '79. Later bikes also had halogen headlight bulbs, though the bulb will have probably been replaced several times in the bike's life. Whatever the age, look for a tarnished or rusted reflector, which is an MOT failure. Reflectors, bulbs, glass and headlight shells are all available.

There were various styles of rear light: 1959-70, '71-72, and the big squared-off item fitted from 1973 to the end. Most should be available as pattern parts, though one handy modification that doesn't alter the outward appearance in any way is an LED rear/stop light bulb. This is a straight swap for the standard bulb, but won't blow and leave you taillight-less on a dark night.

Headlight reflector in good condition – corrosion will be obvious.

Later, squarer rear light fitted from 1973 – the style varied over the years.

Electrics/wiring

A traditional bête noir of Triumph twins, though the electrical system was updated over the years. The Thunderbird started out with a magneto and dynamo, switching to alternator and contact breaker (cb) points in 1954, but the T110 and TR6 retained a magneto/dynamo until 1960, when they too adopted the alternator. Unit construction in 1963 brought coils and twin cb points.

12-volts replaced six in 1966, with the addition of a zener diode (the finned item hiding beneath the headlight from 1968) to control charging. Another useful improvement in '68 was the Lucas 6CA contact breakers, which allowed independent adjustment of the spark for each cylinder, and thus more accurate timing – however, the real answer to electrical problems is electronic ignition. Meriden fitted that from 1979, along with a beefier three-phase alternator. Both of these were big steps forward, the latter boosting charge at low revs and allowing daytime headlight running.

However, the electrical system still needs checking. A good general indication of the owner's attitude is the condition of the wiring – is it tidy and neat, or flopping around? The many bullet connectors need to be clean and tight, and many odd electrical problems are simply down to bad connections or a poor earth. Up to 1970, bikes came with an ammeter, which at least gives some indication that all is

Electrical faults are often simply down to poor connections.

Alternators are generally reliable.

A faulty rear brake light could be the result of corrosion in the switch.

The zener diode should be securely mounted with good connections.

well in the charging circuit. Early 'ignition' warning lights are there simply to inform you that the ignition is on, not whether the alternator is doing its job.

Finally, check that everything works: lights, horn, indicators (fitted post '71, but sometimes removed by owners) and stop light (water can enter the rear brake switch).

Wheels/tyres

Nearly all of these bikes used spoked wheels with chromed steel rims, though a small number of very late Tiger 750s left the factory with alloy wheels. On the steel wheels, check the chrome condition on the rims – rechroming entails a complete dismantle and rebuild of the wheel. Check that none of the spokes are loose, and give each one a gentle tap with a screwdriver – any that are 'off key' will need retensioning. Alloy wheels should be checked for cracks, though there's no evidence that they are prone to them.

Tyres should have at least the

Any loose or bent spokes will have to be replaced.

legal minimum of tread. That's at least 1mm of tread depth across at least three-quarters of the breadth of the tyre. Or if the tread doesn't reach that far across the breadth (true of some modern tyres) then any tread showing must be at least 1mm deep. Beware of bikes that have been left standing (especially on the side stand) for some time, allowing the tyres to crack and deteriorate – it's no reason to reject the bike, but it's a good bargaining tool. New tyres in suitable sizes are no problem at all.

Worn tyres are a good bargaining tool.

Wheel bearings

4 3 2 1

Wheel bearings aren't expensive, but fitting them is a hassle, and if there's play it could affect the handling. To check them, put the bike on its centre stand, put the steering on full lock and try rocking the front wheel in a vertical plane, then spin the wheel and listen for signs of roughness. Do the same for the rear wheel.

Play in worn wheel bearings shows up in lateral movement at the wheel rim ...

... same story at the front.

Steering head bearings

4 3 2 1

Again, the bearings don't cost and arm or leg, but trouble here can affect the handling, and changing them is a big job. With the bike on the centre stand, swing the handlebars from lock to lock. They should move freely, with no hint of roughness or stiff patches – if there is, budget for replacements. To check for play, put the steering on full lock, grip the front wheel and try rocking it back and forth.

Swing arm bearings

4 3 2 1

Another essential for good handling is the swing arm bearings. These should have been regularly greased, and if they haven't, rapid wear or even seizure can result, the latter if the bike has been left

Swing arm bearings live under this grease nipple. Replacing them is a big job.

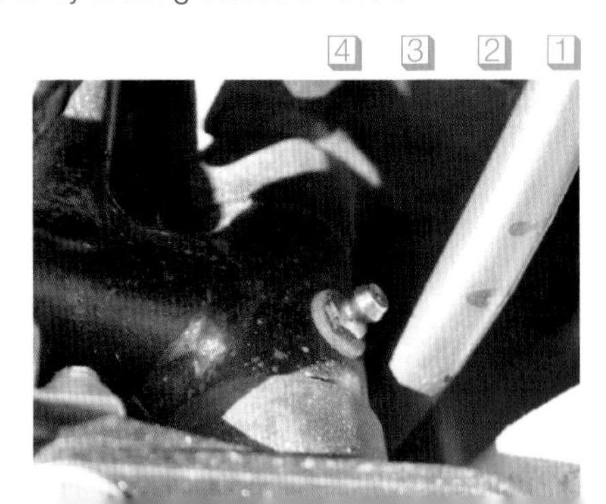

standing for some time. To check for wear, get hold of the rear end of the arm on one side and try rocking the complete swing arm from side-to-side. There should be no perceptible movement.

Suspension

4 3  

With one exception, all these single-carb Triumphs used the same basic suspension setup: front telescopic forks and twin rear dampers, which were later adjustable. The forks were fully shrouded on the Thunderbird and T110, but all Trophys and Tigers used rubber gaiters.

From '71, to go with the new oil-bearing frame, Ceriani-type forks with exposed stanchions were fitted. These did a good job, but suffered from exposure to the elements, and gaiters were reintroduced on UK-spec Tigers in 1973 – US machines (also offered in Britain, confusingly enough) stuck with the sexier exposed forks. The rear shocks didn't lose their shrouding until 1969, and then stayed that way, with chrome springs, until the very end. Until 1955, the rigid Thunderbird used the sprung hub in place of a swingarm and twin shocks. Peculiar to Triumph, this incorporated springs inside the rear hub, which delivered a very limited amount (just over two inches) of suspension travel. If looking at a sprung hub, check that it is moving, but overhaul is a specialist job.

Shrouded shocks on the Thunderbird.

1969-on shock with exposed spring – replacements are readily available.

Check forks for play and oil leaks.

Check both forks and rear shocks for leaks. The fork stanchions chrome plate eventually pits, especially when exposed to the elements and/or the bike has been used in winter. When that happens, it rapidly destroys the oil seals – hence the leaks. New stanchions, or reground and replated existing ones, are the answer, as there's little point in fitting new seals to rough forks.

Check for play by grabbing the bottom of the forks and trying to rock them back and forth; play here indicates worn bushes. Worn out rear shocks will manifest themselves as a weave over 70mph, and sick forks will likewise spoil the bike's handling.

Instruments

4 3 2 1

Instruments are what you would expect from a British bike. The Thunderbird and T110 had nacelle-mounted speedometer and ammeter, and the TR6 Trophy a separate speedo with ammeter mounted in the headlight shell. A tachometer was optional on the TR6 from 1957 right up to 1970, though many bikes have been fitted with one. From 1971, the ammeter was dropped and all bikes had speedo and tacho.

There were various styles, depending on year, but Triumph instruments didn't change as frequently as the rest of the bike, with grey-faced matching Smiths speedo and rev counter replaced by black-faced ones in 1971, and finally by French-made Veglia units.

A speedo check obviously has to wait for the test ride – if nothing is working, the cable is the most likely culprit, but if either the mileometer or speedo have ceased to function while the other is still working, then there's something wrong internally. Instrument repair is best left to a specialist. A battered and bent chrome bezel suggests that a previous owner has had a go themselves.

Early 1970s style speedometer and tachometer.

Late-style instruments, with original Smiths tacho and replacement Veglia speedo.

Both the Thunderbird and T110 included speedo and ammeter in the nacelle.

Engine/gearbox – general impression    

You can tell a lot about the likely condition of a Triumph twin without hearing it run. These engines are easy to work on, and the drawback of that is that it encourages keen and/or impecunious owners to take things apart themselves, often without the proper tools. Look for 'chewed up' screw or Allen bolt heads, and rounded off bolts, plus damage to the casings surrounding them.

It's part of motorcycling folklore that old Triumphs leak oil, but it's not necessarily the case. As long as the engine is in good condition and has been properly put

A first look at the engine and gearbox can give a useful indication of condition.

Have the Allen screws and bolts been rounded off by badly-fitting tools?

together, it should be reasonably oil tight, certainly in the case of the later 750s. Some light misting isn't a bad sign, but if the bike has a puddle of oil underneath it, and the engine/gearbox is covered in lubricant, then walk away – unless, of course, the price reflects the condition. An engine like that is likely to need a complete rebuild.

Triumph engines will carry on running when in very poor condition. One professional restorer I know was given a unit to rebuild. He found that a previous owner had chrome-plated the crank journals and cam bearings, which had then broken up. One con rod was cracked and three of the pushrods were bent. It was also a 'bitsa' engine, made up of random parts: a '64 bottom end with a '71 cylinder head, one 'R' spec cam follower and three standard ones. In the UK, that engine cost x4000 to rebuild.

Many of the same comments apply to the gearbox – look for chewed fasteners and signs of neglect. Remove the oil filler cap and stick a finger inside to check whether the oil has been changed recently – nice clean EP90 … or a frothy sludge.

Triumphs don't *have* to leak oil – check all over the engine and gearbox after your test ride.

Pre-unit engine (actually a Bonneville) showing signs of long neglect …

4 3 2 1

Engine – starting/idling

Triumph engines are good starters, and one in good condition should fire up within two or three kicks. If it doesn't, there's something wrong. The most likely culprit (if electronic ignition hasn't been fitted) is simply maladjusted contact breaker points and ignition timing. A more serious cause is poor compression, which indicates general wear that will need a top end rebuild to rectify. Take a compression tester along, and use it.

Electric start bikes had their teething troubles, which should now have been overcome, and the starter should engage cleanly without excessive noise. About half the 1981-82 machines were fitted with push-button starting, but this amounts to only around 200 Tiger 750s.

Once started, the engine should idle evenly on both cylinders. If it sounds and feels lumpy and uneven, then contact breaker or carburettor adjustments are the most likely

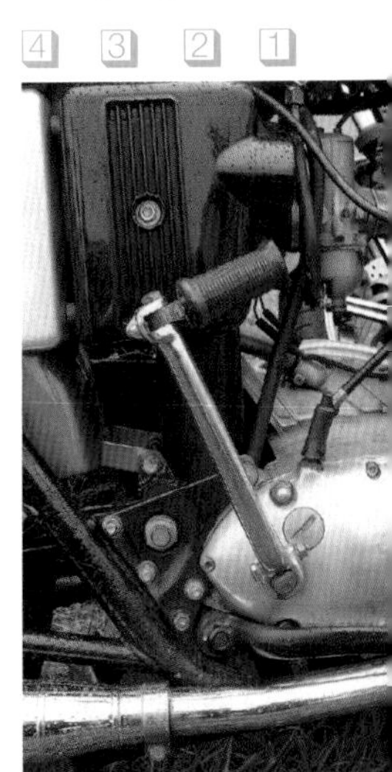

Kickstart needs only a modicum of technique … the engine should start readily.

cause, but a knowledgeable owner should already have these spot-on. If the carburettor is worn, both new parts and complete carbs are available. Another possible cause of uneven idling and running is damage to the hoses connecting the carburettor to the air filter and inlet stub – this can cause air leaks and upset the mixture. A few Tigers have been fitted with modern Mikuni carburettors to replace the Amal, which is said to improve both starting and performance.

Electric start should engage cleanly.

Engine – smoke/noise

4 3 2 1

If you're used to quiet, smooth, modern water-cooled motorcycles, don't be alarmed by the merry clattering emanating from the Triumph's rocker boxes, as they all do that. Even among old British bikes, the Triumph twin had a reputation for mechanical noise from the top end. Adjusting the tappets is an easy enough job, though access is far easier on the '73-on bikes, with their full-width rocker box covers.

A sign of real trouble is knocking or rumbling from the bottom end, which will mean a complete engine rebuild for sure. Whether it's big-ends or mains that need attention, the cure is engine out and a complete strip to find out what's wrong. Beware of impressively loud megaphone silencers that may mask the more subtle knockings of a sick bottom end. Don't buy a bike that's making these noises unless it's cheap. Engine parts to cure all of this are no problem at all, for all bikes.

This much blue smoke suggests piston/ bore and or valve/guide wear.

Look back at the silencers and blip the throttle. Blue smoke means the engine is burning oil and is a sign of general wear in the top end. That means a rebore (again, parts, including oversize pistons, are available), but inevitably other problems will come up once the engine is apart – the valves and guides will probably need replacing as well. Black smoke, indicating rich running, is less of a problem, caused by carburettor wear or (fingers crossed) simply a blocked air filter. Bikes without air filters should be avoided, as you don't know what nasties the motor has ingested.

Listen for rumbling from the primary drive.

Some valve noise from the top end is normal.

Primary drive

Listen to the primary drive while the engine is running. Noises from this area – clonks or rumbles – could be due to a number of things. It could be wear in the clutch and its shock absorber, the engine sprocket chattering on worn splines, or the alternator rotor coming loose on the crank's driving shaft. Of course, you won't know which without taking the primary drive cover off, but if the seller acknowledges that a noise is there, it's another good lever to reduce the price.

Noises in the primary drive indicate clutch or alternator trouble.

Primary chains on pre-unit bikes (up to 1962) are prone to rapid wear, thanks to less effective lubrication. In theory, the unit construction bikes' primary chain, running in its nice clean oil bath, should have a much longer life, but should still be checked regularly. Adjustment of the chain tensioner, through the drain plug hole, is messy and awkward (though easier with the proper tool), and may have been neglected.

Chain/sprockets

4 3 2 1

With the engine switched off, examine the final drive chain and sprockets. Is the chain clean, well lubed and properly adjusted? The best way to check how worn it is is to take hold of a link and try to pull it rearwards away from the sprocket. It should reveal only a small portion of the sprocket teeth – any more and it needs replacing.

Check the rear sprocket teeth for wear – if they have a hooked appearance, the sprocket needs replacing. Ditto if any teeth are damaged or missing. And if the rear sprocket needs replacing, then the gearbox sprocket will too. Chain and sprockets aren't massively expensive, but changing the gearbox sprocket takes some dismantling time.

Worn sprockets mean a new chain is needed too.

Battery

4 3 2 1

Hinge up the seat and check the battery (or in the case of early 12-volt bikes, twin 6-volt batteries). Acid splashes indicate overcharging. The correct electrolyte level is a good sign of a meticulous owner, and do check that the battery is securely kept in place by its rubber strap. If it isn't, the battery can leap upwards over bumps and short out against the metal seat base. (Again, author's experience).

Is the battery secure and topped-up?

Engine/gearbox mountings

4 3 2 1

These need to be completely solid, with no cracks, and no missing or loose bolts – if not, the bike is not in a rideable

Engine and gearbox mounts, whether bolted or welded to the frame, should be solid.

condition. The exact design changed over the years (some were welded to the frame, some bolted) but the points to check are the same.

Exhaust

All bikes left the factory with twin silencers (high-level on the TR6 and TR6C) though some have since been fitted with aftermarket two-into-one systems. These save a little weight and make chain adjustment (both primary and rear) easier. From 1969, all bikes had a balance pipe between the downpipes.

Replacement silencers are available.

Downpipes should be secure in the cylinder head.

Check that the downpipes are secure in the cylinder head (looseness causes air leaks) and examine all joints for looseness and leaks, all of which are MOT failures. The silencers should be secure, firmly mounted and in solid condition. Replacements for the various types are all available.

Test ride

The test ride should be not less than 15 minutes, and you should be doing the riding – not the seller riding with you on the pillion. It's understandable that some sellers are reluctant to let a complete stranger loose on their pride and joy, but it does go with the territory of selling a bike, and so long as you leave an article of faith (usually the vehicle you arrived in) then a test ride is a reasonable request. Take your driving licence in case the seller wants to see it.

Main warning lights

All Triumphs have an ignition warning light, but on early bikes this only serves to tell you that the ignition is on – it doesn't warn of poor charging, which is what the ammeter is for. Don't expect the ammeter to give a foolproof reading at high revs, but so long as it shows a positive charge with the lights on at moderate revs, all is well. Tiger 750s had

Oil light (fitted to Tiger 750s) should flicker out over idling speed.

a conventional ignition light, which should flicker out once revs are over idling speed. Ditto the oil pressure warning light, which the 650cc bikes didn't have, though this isn't infallible.

On bikes up to 1978, warning lights are mounted in the headlight shell, and from '79, they moved to a separate cluster between the speedometer and rev counter. These later bikes also have a neutral light, though it's not a perfect guide, and most riders still find neutral by feel.

Engine performance

4 3 2 1

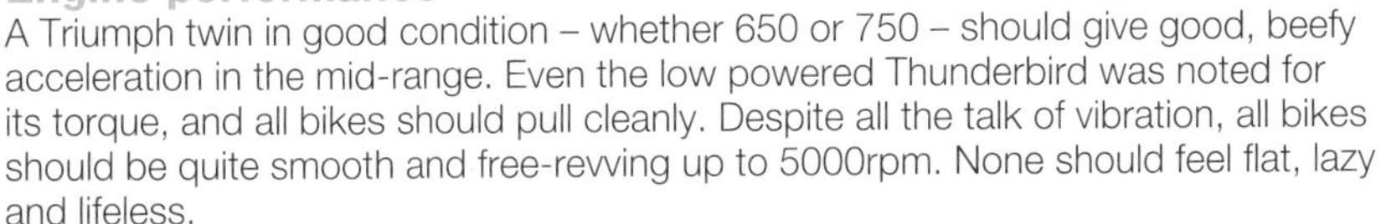

A Triumph twin in good condition – whether 650 or 750 – should give good, beefy acceleration in the mid-range. Even the low powered Thunderbird was noted for its torque, and all bikes should pull cleanly. Despite all the talk of vibration, all bikes should be quite smooth and free-revving up to 5000rpm. None should feel flat, lazy and lifeless.

Ready for the road ... a good Trophy or Tiger (this is an early Bonneville) should give strong performance.

Triumph twins should pull hard and cleanly if all is well.

Check for hesitation, which shouldn't happen – a bike with well set-up ignition and carburetion will pull crisp and clean. Spitting back through the carb can be caused by the absence of an air filter, and the bike should be quite tractable at low speeds, without jerks or hesitation.

If possible, cruise the bike at 60-70mph for five minutes, then check for oil leaks – there shouldn't be anything more than a slight misting. The maximum comfortable cruising speed is around 75mph, partly down to the riding position on Tiger 750s (especially those with US-spec high bars) but also because vibration becomes intrusive over 5000rpm. All of these bikes except the Thunderbird would crack 100mph when new, but they weren't designed for the motorway age (even if some were made then), so it's unfair to expect them to hold modern motorway speeds without ill effects for both machine and rider.

Clutch operation

4 3 2 1

The clutch is heavier than on many modern bikes, but take up should be smooth and positive. Nor should it drag or slip, despite the tales of all Triumph clutches dragging. To check this, select first gear from a standstill. A small crunch is normal, but a full-blooded graunch, followed by a leap forward, means the clutch is dragging. However, the cure is usually down to careful adjustment rather than the wholesale replacement of parts.

Gearbox operation

4 3 2 1

Triumph gearboxes – in both 4-speed 650s and 5-speed 750s – work well, with a clean, positive shift. Watch for stiffness, notchiness and whining. They're also reliable, and, given regular oil changes, should not give trouble. Difficulty in finding neutral at a standstill is not inevitable, so long as the clutch has been set up correctly, so reluctance here is no reason to suspect the bike, though it's often easier to slip into neutral just as you roll to a standstill. However, false neutrals, or slipping out of gear, are sure signs of trouble.

Handling

4 3 2 1

Triumph's reputation for making good handling bikes, especially from the mid-1960s onwards, was well deserved, and the same holds true today. Bear in mind, though, that early bikes, especially the pre-units, are not as surefooted at high speeds as the later machines. If you're used to modern suspension, the rigid-frame Thunderbird will seem very sensitive to mid-corner bumps.

These are relatively light bikes with stiff suspension, easy to flick through corners, and highly agile, so any vagueness and weaving is usually down to worn forks, rear shocks or tyres – it's not inherent. They should never feel soft and wallowy – if they do, the suspension condition is your first thing to recheck. Early Tiger 750s suffered from a lack of ground clearance on the left-hand side (the centre stand is the culprit) though this should only worry hard riders.

Brakes

4 3 2 1

Brakes changed hugely during production. The Thunderbird started out with small seven-inch front brake, later

The 1971-72 twin leading-shoe conical hub drum doesn't have a good reputation.

updated with the T110's superior eight-inch item with an air scoop – the TR6 had this brake from the start. Even these brakes weren't really up to the demands of a 100mph machine. Add-in modern traffic conditions, and you need to bear the brakes in mind when riding one of these, and not expect modern disc performance on the test ride.

Things improved dramatically from 1966, with a 44 per cent increase in front brake lining area. These brakes do match past performance, especially the twin leading-shoe front drum from 1968, and they should be smooth and progressive. The 'conical hub' drums fitted in 1971-72 are less well thought of, and spongy in operation.

A front disc arrived in 1973, the rear following in '77. The discs were chrome-plated, which can chew up pads and dramatically shorten their life as the chrome deteriorates. Modern sintered pads are not recommended with the chrome, as they destroy the plating. If the chrome is still there, it's a good idea to have this skimmed off, which avoids all of these problems. On the test ride, check that both disc brakes work well without feeling soft or spongy.

The introduction of a front disc brake was a great improvement.

Late 1960s twin leading-shoe front drum is well respected, and a popular upgrade for earlier bikes.

Cables

4 3 2 1

All the control cables – brakes, throttle and choke – should work smoothly without stiffness or jerking. Poorly lubricated, badly adjusted cables are an indication of general neglect, and the same goes for badly routed cables.

Check brake/clutch/speedo cables are undamaged and well-routed.

Switchgear

4 3 2 1

Like the brakes, switchgear changed many times over the long production run. Early machines were simple in the extreme, with a rotary lighting switch, plus cut-out and horn buttons on the handlebars or headlight nacelle. The lighting switch later became a toggle in the headlight shell, and the 1971 new generation sported

Final switchgear was simple, but effective.

1971-73 Lucas switches are unlabelled, and vulnerable to water ingress.

new Lucas alloy switches (confusingly unlabelled at first). Updated Lucas switches arrived for 1977, and the final bikes used Magura switchgear.

Whatever is fitted, check that it works positively and reliably – early Lucas alloy switches could let in water, with inevitable results. Malfunctioning switches are usually a simple problem to solve, but another reason to bargain over price.

Evaluation procedure

Add up the total points.

Score: 136 = excellent; 102 = good; 68 = average; 34 = poor. Bikes scoring over 95 will be completely usable and will require only maintenance and care to preserve condition. Bikes scoring between 34 and 69 will require some serious work (at much the same cost regardless of score). Bikes scoring between 70 and 94 will require very careful assessment of the necessary repair/restoration costs in order to arrive at a realistic value.

VISIT VELOCE ON THE WEB – WWW.VELOCE.CO.UK
All current books • New book news • Special offers • Gift vouchers • Forum

10 Auctions
– sold! Another way to buy your dream

Auction pros & cons

Pros

Prices will usually be lower than those of dealers or private sellers and you might grab a real bargain on the day. Auctioneers have usually established clear title with the seller. At the venue you can usually examine documentation relating to the bike.

Cons

You have to rely on a sketchy catalogue description of condition and history. The opportunity to inspect is limited and you cannot ride the bike. Auction machines can be a little below par and may require some work. It's easy to overbid. There will usually be a buyer's premium to pay in addition to the auction hammer price.

Which auction?

Auctions by established auctioneers are advertised in the motorcycle magazines and on the auction houses' websites. A catalogue, or a simple printed list of the lots for auction might only be available a day or two ahead, though often lots are listed and pictured on auctioneers' websites much earlier. Contact the auction company to ask if previous auction selling prices are available, as this is useful information (details of past sales are often available on websites).

Catalogue, entry fee and payment details

When you purchase the catalogue of the bikes in the auction, it often acts as a ticket allowing two people to attend the viewing days and the auction. Catalogue details tend to be comparatively brief, but will include information such as "one owner from new, low mileage, full service history," etc. It will also usually show a guide price to give you some idea of what to expect to pay and will tell you what is charged as a 'buyer's premium.' The catalogue will also contain details of acceptable forms of payment. At the fall of the hammer an immediate deposit is usually required, the balance payable within 24 hours. If the plan is to pay by cash there may be a cash limit. Some auctions will accept payment by debit card. Sometimes credit or charge cards are acceptable, but will often incur an extra charge. A bank draft or bank transfer will have to be arranged in advance with your own bank as well as with the auction house. No bike will be released before all payments are cleared. If delays occur in payment transfers then storage costs can accrue.

Buyer's premium

A buyer's premium will be added to the hammer price: don't forget this in your calculations. It is not usual for there to be a further state tax or local tax on the purchase price and/or on the buyer's premium.

Viewing

In some instances it's possible to view on the day, or days before, as well as in the hours prior to, the auction. There are auction officials available who are willing to help out if need be. While the officials may start the engine for you, a test ride is out of the question. Examining the bike as much as you want is permitted. You can also ask to see any documentation available.

Bidding

Before you take part in the auction, decide your maximum bid – and stick to it!

It may take a while for the auctioneer to reach the lot you are interested in, so use that time to observe how other bidders behave. When it's the turn of your bike, attract the auctioneer's attention and make an early bid. The auctioneer will then look to you for a reaction every time another bid is made. Usually the bids will be in fixed increments until the bidding slows, when smaller increments will often be accepted before the hammer falls. If you want to withdraw from the bidding, make sure the auctioneer understands your intentions – a vigorous shake of the head when he or she looks to you for the next bid should do the trick!

Assuming that you are the successful bidder, the auctioneer will note your card or paddle number, and from that moment on you will be responsible for the bike.

If it is unsold, either because it failed to reach the reserve or because there was little interest, it may be possible to negotiate with the owner, via the auctioneers, after the sale is over.

Successful bid

There are two more items to think about – how to get the bike home, and insurance. If you can't ride it, your own or a hired trailer is one way, another is to have it shipped using the facilities of a local company. The auction house will also have details of companies specialising in the transport of bikes.

Insurance for immediate cover can usually be purchased on site, but it may be more cost-effective to make arrangements with your own insurance company in advance, and then call to confirm the full details.

eBay & other online auctions?

eBay and other online auctions once had a reputation for bargains, though many traders as well as private sellers now use eBay and prices have risen. As with any auction, the final price depends how many buyers are bidding and how desperately they want the bike!

Either way, it would be foolhardy to bid without examining the bike first, which is something most vendors encourage. A useful feature of eBay is that the geographical location of the bike is shown, so you can narrow your choices to those within a realistic radius of home. Be prepared to be outbid in the last few moments of the auction. Remember, your bid is binding and that it will be very, very difficult to get restitution in the case of a crooked vendor fleecing you – caveat emptor! Look at the seller's rating as well as the bike.

Be aware that some bikes offered for sale in online auctions are 'ghost' machines. Don't part with any cash without being sure that the vehicle does actually exist and is as described (usually pre-bidding inspection is possible).

Auctioneers

Bonhams www.bonhams.com/ British Car Auctions (BCA) www.bca-europe.com or www.british-car-auctions.co.uk/ Cheffins www.cheffins.co.uk/ eBay www.eBay.com/ H&H www.classic-auctions.co.uk/ Shannons www.shannons.com.au/ Silver www.silverauctions.com

11 Paperwork

– correct documentation is essential!

The paper trail

Classic bikes sometimes come with a large portfolio of paperwork accumulated and passed on by a succession of proud owners. This documentation represents the real history of the machine, from which you can deduce how well it's been cared for, how much it's been used, which specialists have worked on it and the dates of major repairs and restorations. All of this information will be priceless to you as the new owner, so be very wary of bikes with little paperwork to support their claimed history.

Registration documents

All countries/states have some form of registration for private vehicles whether its like the American 'pink slip' system or the British 'log book' system.

It is essential to check that the registration document is genuine, that it relates to the bike in question, and that all the details are correctly recorded, including frame and engine numbers (if these are shown). If you are buying from the previous owner, his or her name and address will be recorded in the document: this will not be the case if you are buying from a dealer.

In the UK the current (Euro-aligned) registration document is the V5C, and is printed in coloured sections of blue, green and pink. The blue section relates to the motorcycle specification, the green section has details of the registered keeper (who is not necessarily the legal owner) and the pink section is sent to the DVLA in the UK when the bike is sold. A small section in yellow deals with selling within the motor trade.

In the UK the DVLA will provide details of earlier keepers of the bike upon payment of a small fee, and much can be learned in this way.

If the bike has a foreign registration there may be expensive and time-consuming formalities to complete. Do you really want the hassle? More recently, many of the thousands of Trophys exported to the USA have been re-imported to the UK. It sounds like a great chance to buy a Triumph that has only been used on dry, West Coast roads, with the added glamour of US heritage. Plus the fact that US prices tend to be lower – a good condition late '60s Trophy will sell for around x6000, which is about 40 per cent less than the UK price.

However, you'll have to buy the bike sight unseen, and the paperwork involved in importing and re-registering is a daunting prospect. It means employing a shipping agent and budgeting-in the shipping costs. Then there's (at the time of writing) six per cent import duty on the bike and shipping costs, then 20 per cent VAT on the whole lot. Unless you're after a rare US-only spec bike, it's not worth the hassle.

Roadworthiness certificate

Most country/state administrations require that bikes are regularly tested to prove they are safe to use on the public highway. In the UK that test (the 'MOT') is carried out at approved testing stations, for a fee. In the USA the requirement varies, but most states insist on an emissions test every two years as a minimum, while the police are charged with pulling over unsafe-looking vehicles.

In the UK the test is required on an annual basis for all post-1960 vehicles of more than three years old. Even if it isn't a legal necessity, a conscientious owner can opt to put the bike through the test anyway, as a health check. Of particular relevance for older bikes is that the certificate issued includes the mileage reading recorded at the test date and, therefore, becomes an independent record of that machine's history. Ask the seller if previous certificates are available. Without an MOT the bike should be trailered to its new home, unless you insist that a valid MOT is part of the deal (Not such a bad idea this, as at least you will know the bike was roadworthy on the day it was tested, and you don't need to wait for the old certificate to expire before having the test done).

Road licence

The administration of every country/state charges some kind of tax for the use of its road system – the actual form of the 'road licence' and how it is displayed varying enormously country to country and state to state.

Whatever the form of the road licence, it must relate to the vehicle carrying it and must be present and valid if the bike is to be ridden legally on the public highway. The value of the license will depend on the length of time it will continue to be valid.

In the UK if a bike is untaxed because it has not been used for a period of time, the owner has to inform the licensing authorities, otherwise the vehicle's date-related registration number will be lost and there will be a painful amount of paperwork to get it re-registered. Also in the UK, bikes built before the end of 1973 are road tax exempt, but they must still display a valid disc. Bike clubs can often provide formal proof that a particular machine qualifies for this valuable concession.

Certificates of authenticity

For many makes of classic bike it is possible to get a certificate proving the age and authenticity (eg engine and frame numbers, paint colour and trim) of a particular machine. These are sometimes called 'Heritage Certificates,' and if the bike comes with one of these it is a definite bonus. If you want to obtain one, the owners' club is the best starting point.

Valuation certificate

Hopefully, the vendor will have a recent valuation certificate, or letter signed by a recognised expert stating how much he or she believes the particular bike to be worth (such documents, together with photos, are usually needed to get 'agreed value' insurance). Generally such documents should act only as confirmation of your own assessment of the bike rather than a guarantee of value, as the expert has probably not seen it in the flesh. The easiest way to find out how to obtain a formal valuation is to contact the owners' club.

Service history

Often these bikes will have been serviced at home by enthusiastic (and hopefully capable) owners for a good number of years. Nevertheless, try to obtain as much service history and other paperwork pertaining to the bike as you can. Naturally specialist garage receipts score most points in the value stakes. However, anything helps in the great authenticity game: items like the original bill of sale, handbook, parts invoices, and repair bills adding to the story and the character of the machine.

Even a brochure correct to the year of the bike's manufacture is a useful document, and something that you could well have to search hard to locate in future years. If the seller claims that the bike has been restored, then expect receipts and other evidence from a specialist restorer.

If the seller claims to have carried out regular servicing, ask what work was completed, when, and seek some evidence of it being carried out. Your assessment of the bike's overall condition should tell you whether the seller's claims are genuine.

Restoration photographs

If the seller tells you that the bike has been restored, then expect to be shown a series of photographs taken while the restoration was under way. Pictures taken at various stages, and from various angles, should help you gauge the thoroughness of the work. If you buy the bike, ask if you can have copies of all the photographs, as they form an important part of its history.

VISIT VELOCE ON THE WEB – WWW.VELOCE.CO.UK
All current books • New book news • Special offers • Gift vouchers • Forum

12 What's it worth?

– let your head rule your heart

Condition

If the bike you've been looking at is really ratty, then you've probably not bothered to use the marking system in chapter 9 – 30 minute evaluation. You may not have even got as far as using that chapter at all!

If you did use the marking system, you'll know whether the bike is in excellent (maybe concours), good, average or poor condition, or perhaps somewhere in between these categories.

To keep up to date with prices, buy the latest editions of classic motorcycle magazines, and check the classified and dealer ads, both in the magazines and online – these are particularly useful as they enable you to compare private and dealer prices. Most of the magazines run auction reports as well, which publish the actual selling prices, as do auction house websites. Remember that the price listed for online auctions (unless it's a 'Buy it Now' price) is only the highest current bid, not the final selling price.

There was a time when the single-carburettor Triumphs were significantly cheaper than the equivalent Bonneville. Those days have gone, and prices are now much closer. Pre-unit (up to 1962) bikes tend to fetch the highest prices, closely followed by unit construction bikes up to 1970. 1971-on bikes (this goes for Bonnevilles as well) are cheaper, despite being thinner on the ground. At the time of writing, prices were starting to rise.

Bear in mind that a bike that is truly a recent show winner could be worth more than the highest price usually seen. Assuming that the bike you have in mind is not in show/concours condition, then relate the level of condition that you judge it to be in with the appropriate price in the adverts. How does the figure compare with the asking price?

Before you start haggling with the seller, consider what effect any variation from standard specification might have on the bike's value. This is a personal thing. For some, absolute originality is non-negotiable, while others see non-standard parts as an opportunity to pick up a bargain. Do your research in the reference books, so that you know the bike's spec when it left the factory. That way, you shouldn't end up paying a top-dollar price for a non-original bike. If you are buying from a dealer, remember prices are generally higher than in private sales.

Striking a deal

Negotiate on the basis of your condition assessment, mileage, and fault rectification cost. Also take into account the bike's specification. Be realistic about the value, but don't be completely intractable: a small compromise on the part of the vendor or buyer will often facilitate a deal at little real cost.

13 Do you really want to restore?

– it'll take longer and cost more than you think

Temptingly complete, but how long might it take to restore?

There's a romance about restoration projects, about bringing a sick bike back into blooming health, and it's tempting to buy something that 'just needs a few small jobs' to bring it up to scratch. But there are two things to think about. One, once you've got the bike home and start taking it apart, those few small jobs could turn into big ones. Two, restoration takes time, which is a precious thing in itself. Be honest with yourself – will you get as much pleasure from working on the bike as you will from riding it?

Of course, you could hand the whole lot over

Parts missing, non-standard bits – this pre-unit (Bonneville, not Trophy) could prove a challenge.

A ground-up rebuild like this will take time – and will cost.

to a professional, and the biggest cost involved in this case is not the new parts, but the sheer labour involved. Such restorations don't come cheap, and if taking this route there are four other issues to bear in mind as well.

First, make it absolutely clear what you want doing. Do you want the bike to be 100 per cent original at the end of the process, or simply usable? Do you want a concours finish, or are you prepared to put up with a few blemishes on the original parts?

Secondly, make sure that not only is a detailed estimate involved, but that it is more-or-less binding. There are too many stories of a person quoted one figure, only to be presented with an invoice for a far larger one!

Third, check that the company you're dealing with has a good reputation – the owners club, or one of the reputable parts suppliers, should be able to make a few recommendations.

Dismantling may reveal fresh horrors, such as this chewed up crankcase.

Finally, having a Triumph professionally restored is unlikely to make financial sense, as it will probably cost more than the finished bike will be worth. Not that this should put you off, if you have the budget.

Restoring a bike yourself requires a number of skills, which is fine if you already have them, but if you haven't, it's good not to make your newly acquired bike part of the learning curve! Can you weld? Are you confident about building up an engine? Do you have a warm, well-lit garage with a solid workbench and good selection of tools?

Be prepared for a top-notch professional to put you on a lengthy waiting list or, if tackling a restoration yourself, expect things to go wrong, and set aside extra time to complete the task. Restorations can stretch into years when things like life intrude, so it's good to have some sort of target date.

There's a lot to be said for a rolling restoration, especially as the summers start to pass with your bike still off the road. This is not the way to achieve a concours finish, which can only really be achieved via a thorough nut-and-bolt rebuild, without the bike getting wet, gritty and salty in the meantime, but an 'on-the-go' restoration does have its plus points. Riding helps keep your interest up as the bike's condition improves, and it's also more affordable than trying to do everything in one go. In the long run, it will take longer, but you'll get some on-road fun out of the bike in the meantime.

14 Paint problems

– bad complexion, including dimples, pimples and bubbles

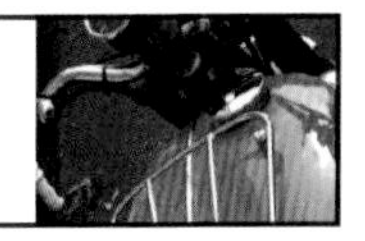

Paint faults generally occur due to lack of protection/maintenance, or to poor preparation prior to a respray or touch-up. Some of the following conditions may be present in the bike you're looking at:

Orange peel

This appears as an uneven paint surface, similar to the appearance of the skin of an orange. The fault is caused by the failure of atomised paint droplets to flow into each other when they hit the surface. It's sometimes possible to rub out the effect with proprietary paint cutting/rubbing compound or very fine grades of abrasive paper. A respray may be necessary in severe cases. Consult a paint shop for advice.

Cracking

Severe cases are likely to have been caused by too heavy an application of paint (or filler beneath the paint). Also, insufficient stirring of the paint before application can lead to the components being improperly mixed, and cracking can result. Incompatibility with the paint already on the panel can have a similar effect. To rectify it is necessary to rub down to a smooth, sound finish before respraying the problem area.

Crazing

Sometimes the paint takes on a crazed rather than a cracked appearance when the problems mentioned under 'cracking' are present. This problem can also be caused by a reaction between the underlying surface and the paint. Paint removal and respraying the problem area is usually the only solution.

Crazing: a subtle, but serious paint fault.

Blistering

Almost always caused by corrosion of the metal beneath the paint. Usually perforation will be found in the metal and the damage will often be worse than that suggested by the area of blistering. The metal will have to be repaired before repainting.

Micro blistering

Usually the result of an economy respray where inadequate heating has allowed moisture to settle on the vehicle before spraying. Consult a paint specialist, but damaged paint will have to be removed before partial or full respraying. Can also be caused by bike covers that don't 'breathe.'

Fading

Some colours, especially reds, are pone to fading if subject to strong sunlight for long periods without the benefit of polish protection. Sometimes proprietary paint restorers and/or paint cutting/rubbing compounds will retrieve the situation. Often a respray is the only real solution.

Fuel stains like this should polish out.

Peeling
Often a problem with metallic paintwork when the sealing lacquer becomes damaged and begins to peel off. Poorly applied paint may also peel. The remedy is to strip and start again.

Dimples
Dimples in the paintwork are caused by the residue of polish (particularly silicone types) not being removed properly before respraying. Paint removal and repainting is the only solution.

Repainting tank badges isn't a big job.

VISIT VELOCE ON THE WEB – WWW.VELOCE.CO.UK
All current books • New book news • Special offers • Gift vouchers • Forum

15 Problems due to lack of use

– just like their owners, Triumph twins need exercise!

Like any piece of engineering, and indeed like human beings, Triumph twins deteriorate if they sit doing nothing for long periods. This is especially relevant if the bike is laid up for six months of the year, as some are.

Rust

If the bike is put away wet, and/or stored in a cold, damp garage, the paint, metal and brightwork will suffer. Ensure the machine is completely dry and clean before going into storage, and if you can afford it, invest in a dehumidifier to keep the garage atmosphere dry.

Rust: the eternal enemy.

Seized components

Pistons in brake calipers can seize partially or fully, giving binding or non-working brakes. Cables are vulnerable to seizure too – the answer is to thoroughly lube them beforehand, and come into the garage to give them a couple of pulls once a week or so.

Tyres

If the bike's been left on its side stand, most of its weight is on the tyres, which will develop flat spots

Give all the levers a pull once a week.

and cracks over time. Always leave the bike on its centre stand, which takes weight off the tyres.

Tyres crack and 'set' over time.

Engine

Old, acidic oil can corrode bearings. Many riders change the oil in the spring, when they're putting the bike back on the road, but really it should be changed just before the bike is laid up, so that the bearings are sitting in fresh oil. The same goes for the gearbox. While you're giving the cables their weekly exercise, turn the engine over slowly on the kickstart, ignition off. Don't start it though – running the engine for a short time does more harm than good, as it produces a lot of moisture internally, which the engine doesn't get hot enough to burn off. That will attack the engine internals and the silencers.

Battery/electrics

Either remove the battery and give it a top-up charge every couple of weeks, or connect it to a battery top-up device, such as the Optimate, which will keep it permanently fully charged. Damp conditions will allow fuses and earth connections to corrode, storing up electrical troubles for the spring. Eventually, wiring insulation will harden and fail.

VISIT VELOCE ON THE WEB – WWW.VELOCE.CO.UK
All current books • New book news • Special offers • Gift vouchers • Forum

16 The Community

– key people, organisations and companies in the Triumph world

Auctioneers

Bonhams www.bonhams.com/
British Car Auctions BCA) www.bca-europe.com or www.british-car-auctions.co.uk/ Cheffins www.cheffins.co.uk/
eBay www.eBay.com/
H&H www.classic-auctions.co.uk/
Shannons www.shannons.com.au/
Silver www.silverauctions.com

Clubs across the world

Triumph Owners Motorcycle Club
The original and longest-lived Triumph club. Offers a bike dating service.
www.tomcc.org

Triumph Owners Motorcycle Club – Germany
www.tomcc.de

Triumph Owners Motorcycle Club – New Zealand
www.tomcc.nz

Triumph International Owners' club – USA
PO Box 158, Plympton, Mass 02367–0158
www.members.aol.com

Triumph Owners Motorcycle Club – Denmark
www.triumphmc.dk

Triumph Owners Motorcycle Club – Netherlands
www.tocn.info

Triumph Owners Motorcycle Club – Belgium
www.tomcc.be

Triumph Owners Motorcycle Club – Norway
www.tomcc-n.com

Triumph Owners Motorcycle Club – Australia
PO Box 257, Belgrave, 3160
www.tomcc.cjb.net
www.tomcc.com.au

Triumph Owners Motorcycle Club – Sweden
www.tomccsweden.org

Club Triton – France
www.triton-france.com

Specialists

There are so many Triumph twin specialists out there that it would be impossible to list them all, and we have restricted our listing to UK companies. This list does not imply recommendation and is not deemed to be comprehensive.

Britbits
Spares – Bournemouth
www.britbits.co.uk - 01202 483675

Burton Bike Bits
Spares – Burton on Trent
www.burtonbikebits.net
01455 841133

Camelford Bike Bits
Spares – Cornwall
01840 213483

Carl Rosner
Spares – London
www.carlrosner.co.uk - 020 8657 0121

High Gear Engine Centre
Engine rebuilds – Surrey
020 8942 2868

Kidderminster Motorcycles
Spares – Herefordshire
01562 66679

Kirby Rowbotham
Electronic ignition/oil filters – Staffordshire
www.kirbyrowbotham.com
01889 584758

LF Harris International
Spares – Devon
Unit 1, Silverhills Road, Decoy Industrial Estate, Newton Abbot, Devon
TQ12 5ND

Morgo
Uprated oil pumps
www.morgo.co.uk

Norman Hyde
Spares – West Midlands
www.normanhyde.co.uk
01926 497375

Reg Allen
Spares – London
www.reg-allen-london.co.uk
020 8579 1248

Robin James Engineering
Restorations – Herefordshire
www.robinjamesengineering.com
01568 612800

Rockerbox
Spares – Surrey
www.rockerbox.co.uk
01252 722973

SRM Engineering
Spares/engineering – Aberystwyth
www.srm-engineering.com
01970 627771

Supreme Motorcycles
Spares – Leicestershire
www.suprememotorcycles.co.uk
01432 820752

The Bike Shed
Restorations/servicing – Hertfordshire
www.thebikeshed.co.uk
01920 830931

TriCor
Spares – Hertfordshire
www.tri-corengland.com
01432 820752

Tri-Supply
Spares – Honiton, Devon
www.trisupply.co.uk
01404 47001

Triumph Bonneville.com
Spares (750cc only)
www.triumphbonneville.com
01743 860146

Unity Equipe
Spares – Lancashire
www.unityequipe.com
01706 632237

Books

British Motorcycles Since 1950 Vols 5 & 6
Steve Wilson, PSL, 1992

Illustrated Triumph Motorcycle Buyers Guide
Roy Bacon, Niton, 1989

The Triumph Trophy Bible
Harry Woolridge, Veloce, 2010

Triumph Pre Unit Twins
Haynes Service & Repair Manual No 0251

Triumph 650 & 750 Unit Twins
Haynes Service & Repair Manual No 0122

Triumph Twin Restoration
Roy Bacon, Osprey, 1985

Triumph Twins & Triples
Roy Bacon, Osprey, 1981

17 Vital statistics

– essential data at your fingertips

Listing the vital statistics of every Thunderbird, T110, Trophy and Tiger variant would take far more room than we have here, so three representative models have been chosen: 1950 Thunderbird, 1961 TR6 Trophy, and 1969 Tiger 650.

Max speed

1950 Thunderbird – 100mph
1961 TR6 – 101mph
1969 Tiger 650 – 101mph

Engine

1959 Thunderbird – Air-cooled vertical twin – 649cc. Bore and stroke 71 x 82mm. Compression ratio 7:1. 34bhp @ 6300rpm
1961 TR6 – Air-cooled vertical twin – 649cc. Bore and stroke 71 x 82mm. Compression ratio 8.5:1. 42bhp @6500rpm
1969 Tiger 650 – Air-cooled vertical twin – 649cc. Bore and stroke 76 x 82mm. Compression ratio 9.0:1. 45bhp @ 6500rpm

Gearbox

1950 Thunderbird – Four-speed. Ratios: 1st 11.2:1, 2nd 7.75:1, 3rd 5.45:1, 4th 4.57:1
1961 TR6 – Four-speed. Ratios: 1st 11.931:1, 2nd 8.27:1, 3rd 5.82:1, 4th 4.89:1
1969 Tiger 650 – Four-speed. Ratios: 1st 11.81:1, 2nd 8.17:1, 3rd 6.04:1, 4th 4.84:1

Brakes

1950 Thunderbird – Cable, 7in front drum, 7in rear drum
1961 TR6 – Cable, 8in front drum, 7in rear drum
1969 Tiger 650 – Cable, 8in twin leading-shoe front drum, 7in rear drum

Electrics

1950 Thunderbird – 6-volt, magneto
1968 T120 – 6-volt, magneto
1969 Tiger 650 – 12-volt, alternator

Weight

1950 Thunderbird – 385lb
1961 TR6 – 400lb
1969 Tiger 650 – 420lb

Major change points by model years

1950 Thunderbird launched
1952 SU carburettor fitted
1954 T110 launched
1956 TR6 Trophy launched, alloy head for T110

1957 Swingarm frame and full-width front hub for Thunderbird, 8in front brake TR6
1958 Slickshift clutchless gear change
1960 Duplex frame, bathtub bodywork for Thunderbird and T110
1961 Strengthened frame, alloy head and 8in front brake for Thunderbird
1962 Larger alternator, heavier flywheel
1963 Unit construction, single downtube frame
1964 New forks, 12v electrics for Thunderbird
1965 Revised forks
1966 New frame geometry, 12-volt electrics, bigger oil tank, bigger front brake
1967 TR6 larger valves, E3134 exhaust cam, 9:1 compression. New oil pump
1968 TLS front brake, 6CA contact breakers, two-way damped forks, braced swingarm, stroboscopic timing cover, finned Zener diode under headlight, Amal Concentric carbs
1969 Heavier flywheel, UNF threads, RM21 alternator, nitrided exhaust cam
1970 New engine breathing system
1971 New generation – oil-in-frame, conical hub drum brakes, Ceriani-style alloy forks, indicators, squared-off UK spec fuel tank, restyled side panels, skimpy mudguards. TR6C and TR6R Tiger 650.
1972 Lowered frame/seat height, five-speed gearbox option, new cylinder head with finned rocker caps
1973 Tiger 750 launched, front disc brake
1974 Lower 7.9:1 compression ratio, US spec offered in UK
1975 No changes due to factory blockade
1976 Left-foot gear change, rear disc brake
1977 Girling gas rear shocks
1978 Improved oil-tightness, Yuasa battery, new seat
1979 Timing-side roller bearing, Lucas Rita electronic ignition, three-phase alternator, new Lucas switchgear, lockable seat, rear parcel rack
1980 Four-valve oil pump, Avon Roadrunner tyres, Electro electric start option
1981 Higher gearing, inlet valve oil seals, twin AP Racing front discs optional, Marzocchi remote reservoir rear shocks. TR65 Thunderbird and Tiger Trail TR7T launched. TR6T later in year.
1982 Rev counter and 2-into-2 exhaust for TR65. Full production ends.
1983 Meriden co-op closes.

Engine/frame numbers

Production for each model year began in August. That is, 1969 model bikes began rolling off the lines in August 1968, after the summer holidays. The numbers below denote the first 650 or 750 twins produced in that model year.

1950	100N	**1958**	011116
1951	101NA	**1959**	020076
1952	15809NA (no suffix from 25000)	**1960**	029364 (later D101)
1953	32303	**1961**	D7727
1954	44135	**1962**	D15789
1955	56700	**1963**	DV101
1956	70930	**1964**	DV5825
1957	0945	**1965**	DV13375

1966	DV24875	**1975**	Up to NJ60070 (650), EK62239 (750)
1967	DV44394	**1976**	HN62501
1968	DV66246	**1977**	GP75000
1969	DV85904	**1978**	HX00100
1970	JD24849	**1979**	HA11001
1971	HE30001	**1980**	PB25001
1972	HG30870	**1981**	KDA28001
1973	JH15366 (650), JH15435, XH22019 (750)	**1982**	EDA30001
1974	GJ55101	**1983**	BEA33001-AEA34393

A 1969 Trophy 650, spotted on a sunny day by the Dorset coast. This could be your bike ...

BUS
978-1-845840-22-8
TR6
978-1-845840-26-6
MGB MGB GT
978-1-845840-29-7
E-type
978-1-845840-77-8
2CV
978-1-845840-99-0
928
978-1-904788-70-6
MINOR & 1000
978-1-845841-01-0
XJ6, XJ12 & Sovereign
978-1-845841-19-5
230, 250 & 280SL
978-1-845841-13-3
GS
978-1-845841-35-5
500 & 650 Twins
978-1-845841-36-2
DS & ID
978-1-845841-38-6
SILVER SHADOW BENTLEY T-SERIES
978-1-845841-46-1
500 & 600
978-1-845841-47-8
IMPREZA
978-1-845841-63-8
Bantam
978-1-845841-65-2
GOLF GTI
978-1-845841-88-1
XJ40
978-1-845841-92-8
XJ
978-1-845842-00-0
MINI
978-1-845842-04-8
CAPRI
978-1-845842-05-5
STAG
978-1-845842-70-3
Commando
978-1-845842-81-9
205 GTI
978-1-845842-83-3
SOHC FOURS
978-1-845842-84-0
TRIPLES & FOURS
978-1-845842-87-1
BONNEVILLE
978-1-84584-134-8
Big Twins
978-1-845843-03-8
CBR600 HURRICANE
978-1-845843-09-0
TR7 & TR8
978-1-845843-16-8
CORVETTE
978-1-845843-29-8
911SC
978-1-845843-30-4
SCOOTERS
978-1-845843-34-2
911 (964)
978-1-845843-38-0
911 (996)
978-1-845843-39-7
XJ-S
978-1-845841-61-4
MX-5 MIATA
978-1-845842-31-4
CBR FireBlade
978-1-845843-07-6
911 (993)
978-1-845843-40-3
SERIES I, II & IIA
978-1-845843-48-9
Bevel Twins
978-1-845843-63-2
924
978-1-845844-09-7

... don't buy a vehicle until you've read one of these!

978-1-845843-52-6

978-1-845843-53-3

978-1-845843-56-4

978-1-845843-54-0

978-1-845843-92-2

978-1-845843-59-5

978-1-845843-60-1

978-1-845843-93-9

978-1-845843-77-9

978-1-845843-91-5

978-1-845844-42-4

978-1-845845-23-0

978-1-845843-95-3

978-1-845844-08-0

978-1-845844-21-9

978-1-845844-22-6

978-1-845844-23-3

978-1-845844-24-0

978-1-845844-30-1

978-1-845844-34-9

978-1-845845-25-4

978-1-845844-43-1

978-1-845844-45-5

978-1-845844-47-9

978-1-845844-56-1

978-1-845844-62-2

978-1-845844-86-8

978-1-845844-87-5

978-1-845845-26-1

978-1-904788-69-0

978-1-845845-33-9

978-1-904788-72-0

978-1-904788-85-0

978-1-845846-09-1

978-1-845844-86-8

978-1-904788-98-0

978-1-845845-71-1

978-1-845846-14-5

978-1-845841-07-2

£9.99 - £12.99 / $19.95
(prices subject to change, p&p extra).

For more details visit
www.veloce.co.uk
or email info@veloce.co.uk

Also from Veloce Publishing ...

– Harry Woolridge –
THE TRIUMPH TROPHY BIBLE
Including unit-construction Trophy-based TIGER models

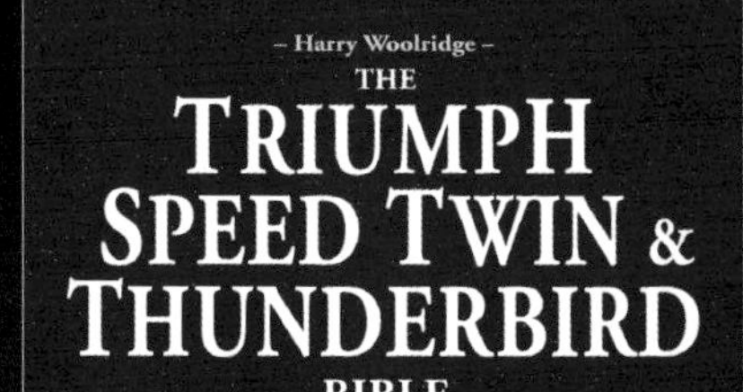

978-1-904788-02-7 • £35.00/$69.95*

978-1-904788-26-3 • £30.00/$59.95*

THE
TRIUMPH
BONNEVILLE
BIBLE
All models 1959-1988
(Does not cover 2001-on models)
PETER HENSHAW

978-1-904788-09-6 • £50.00/$79.95*

978-1-845843-98-4 • £35.00/$54.95*

For more info on Veloce titles, visit our website at www.veloce.co.uk
email: info@veloce.co.uk • Tel: +44(0)1305 260068
*prices subject to change, p&p extra

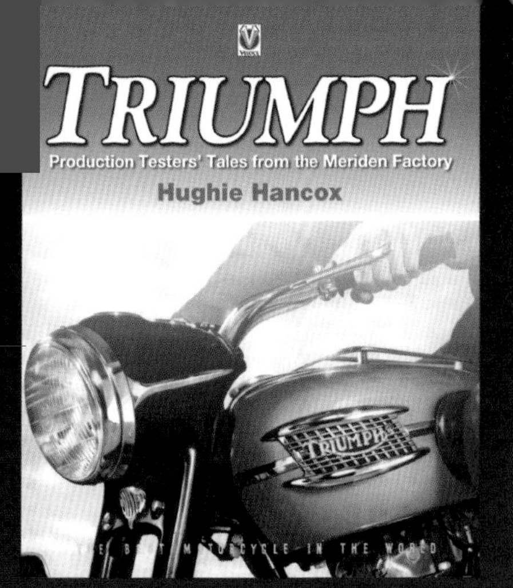

978-1-845844-41-7 • £19.99/$39.95*

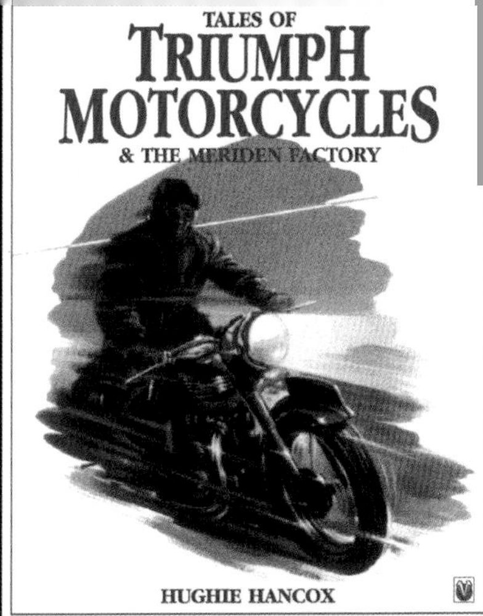

978-1-901295-67-2 • £24.99/$39.95*

Save the
TRIUMPH
BONNEVILLE!
The inside story of the Meriden Workers' Co-op
Foreword by TONY BENN

John Rosamond
(Ex-Chairman Workers' Board of Directors)

978-1-845842-65-9 • £12.49/$24.95*

For more info on Veloce titles, visit our website at www.veloce.co.uk
email: info@veloce.co.uk • Tel: +44(0)1305 260068
* prices subject to change, p&p extra

Index